Kaitlyn's Adult Coloring Book

By Kaitlyn Suter

Color Pallet

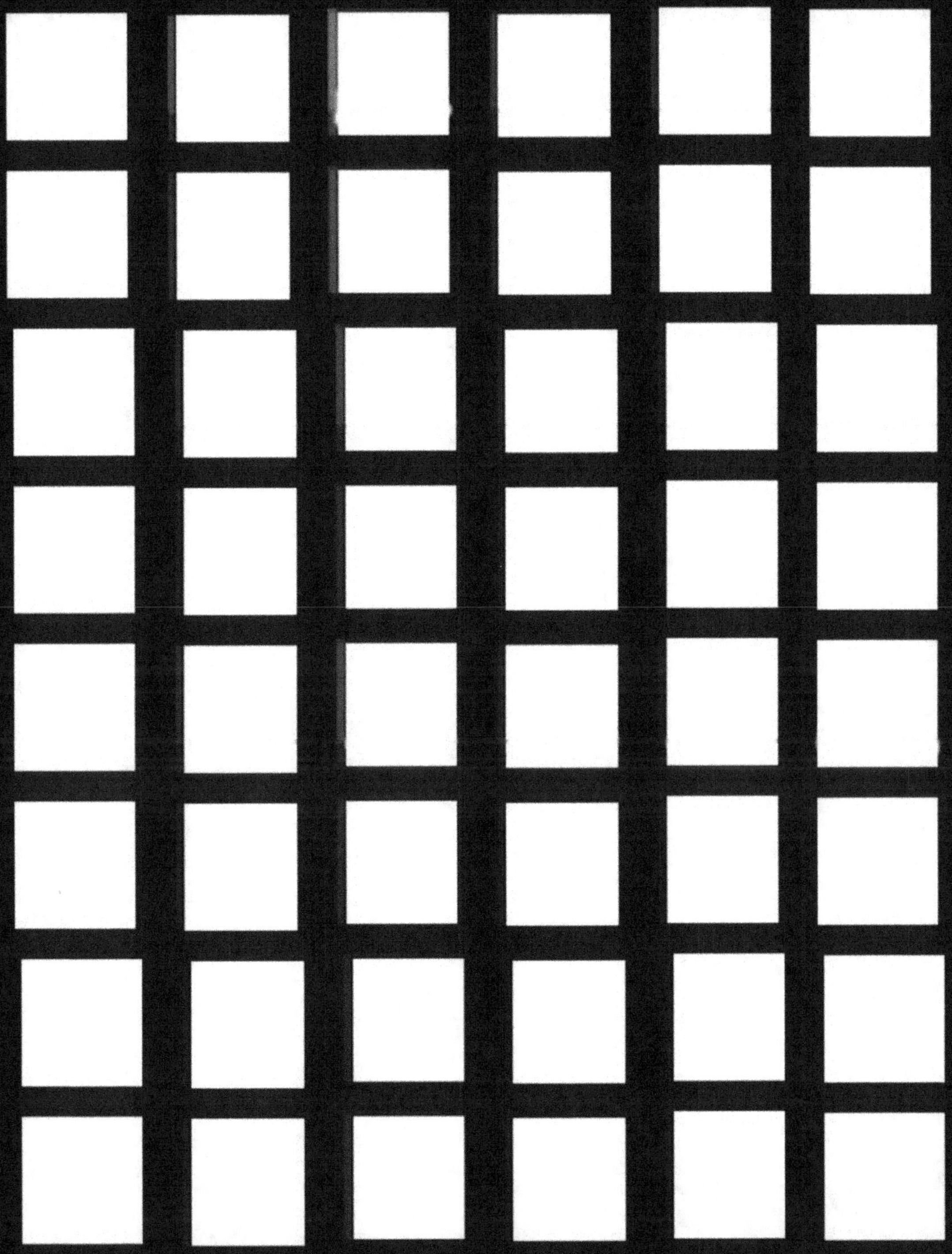

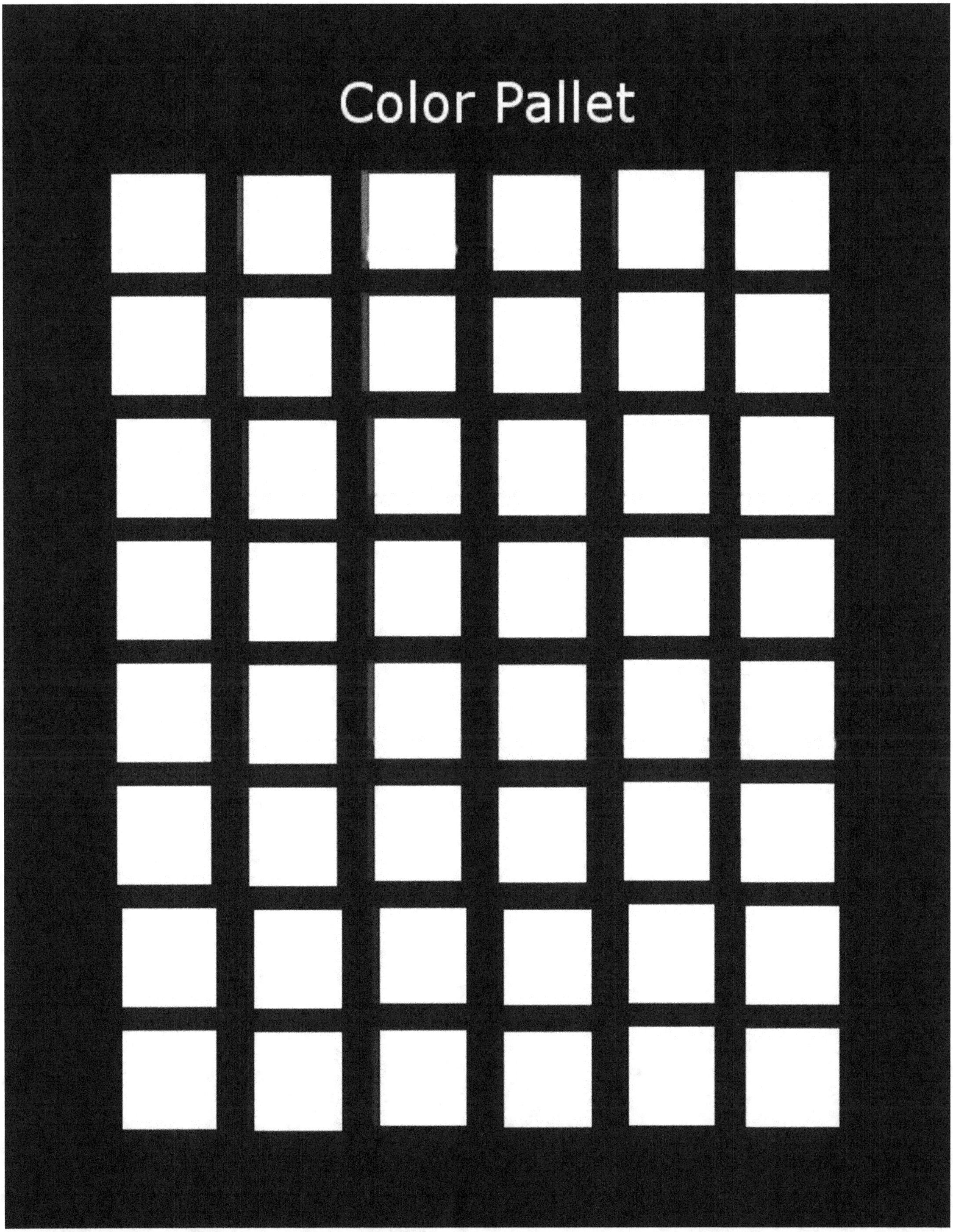
Color Pallet

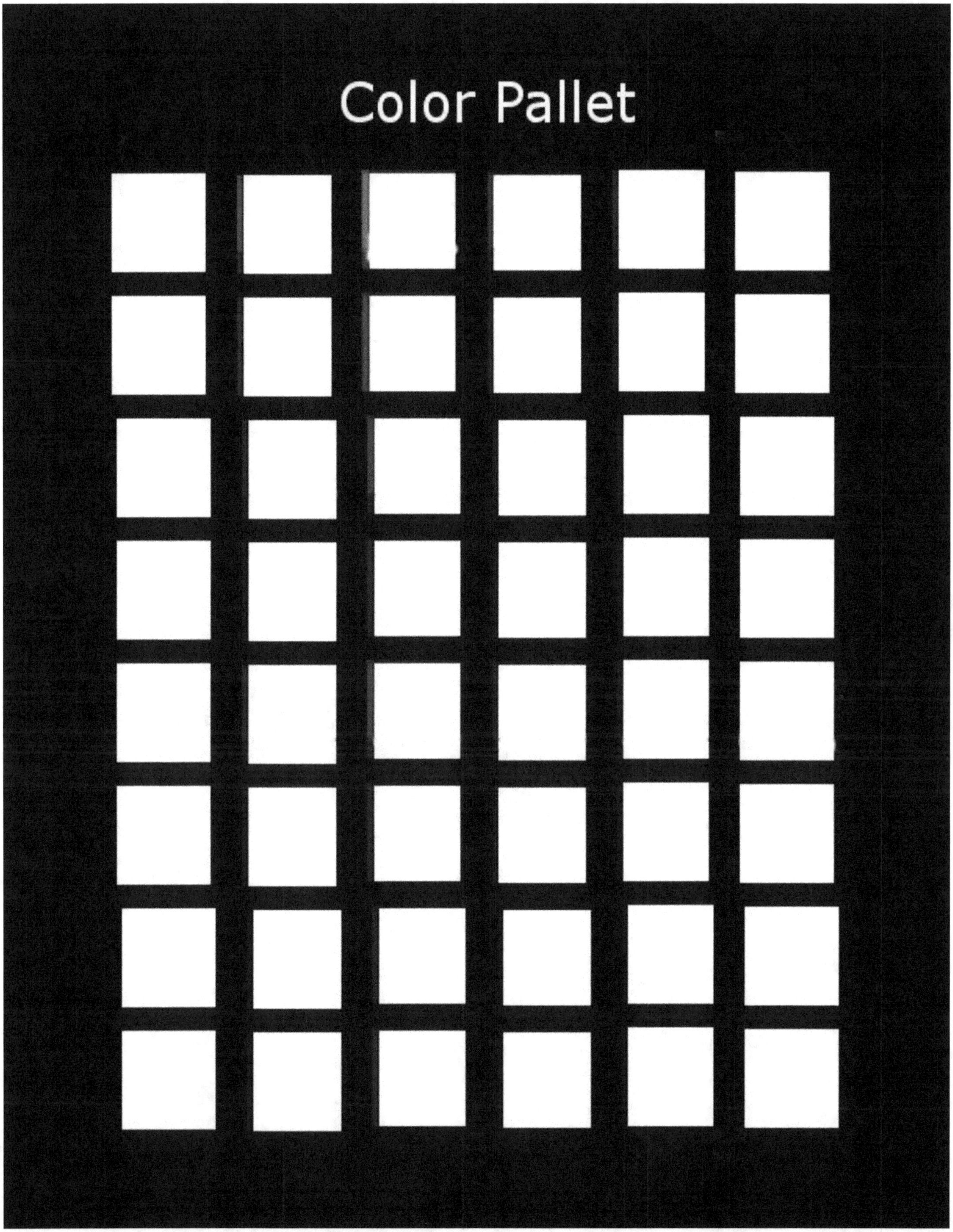
Color Pallet

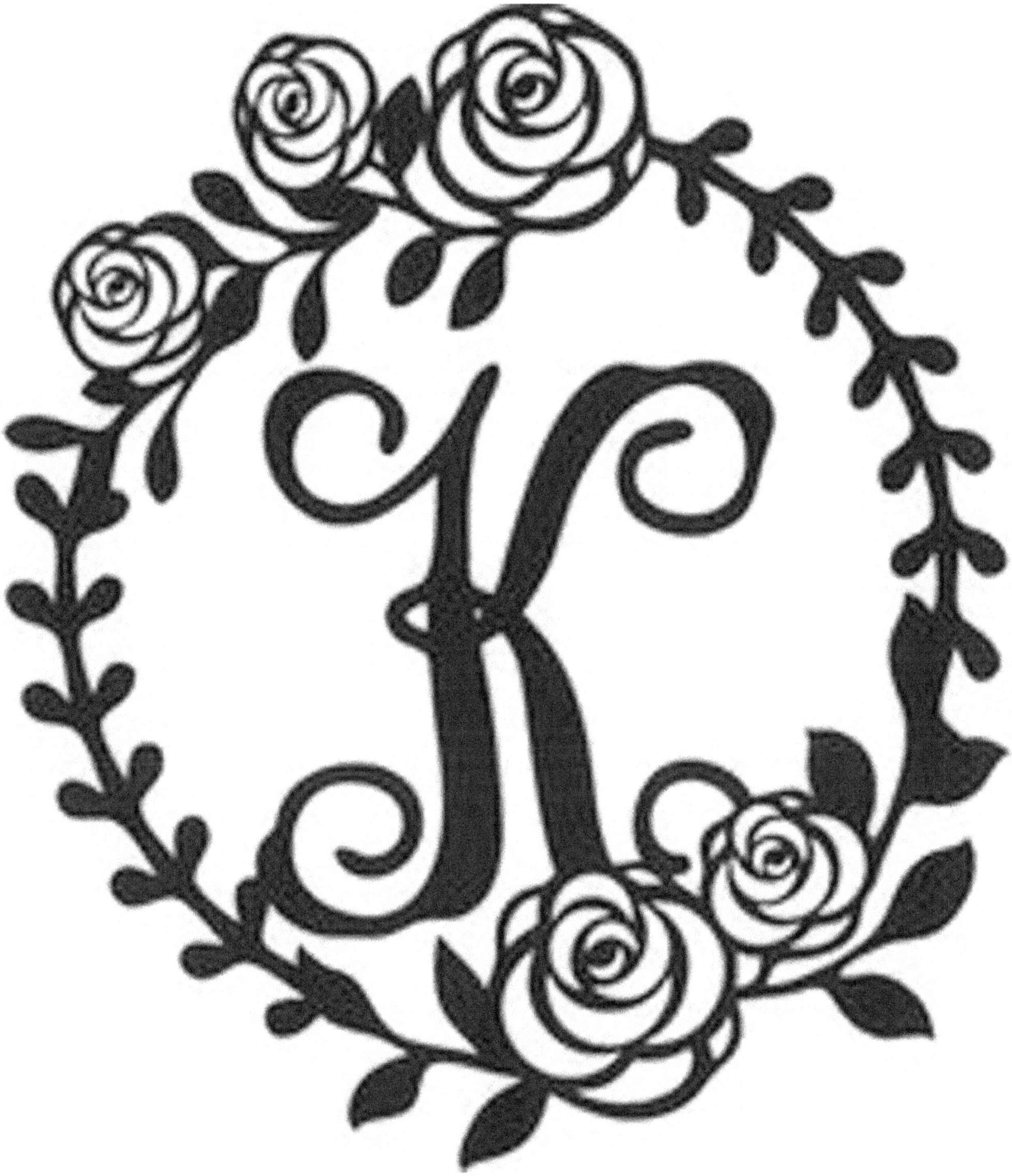
K

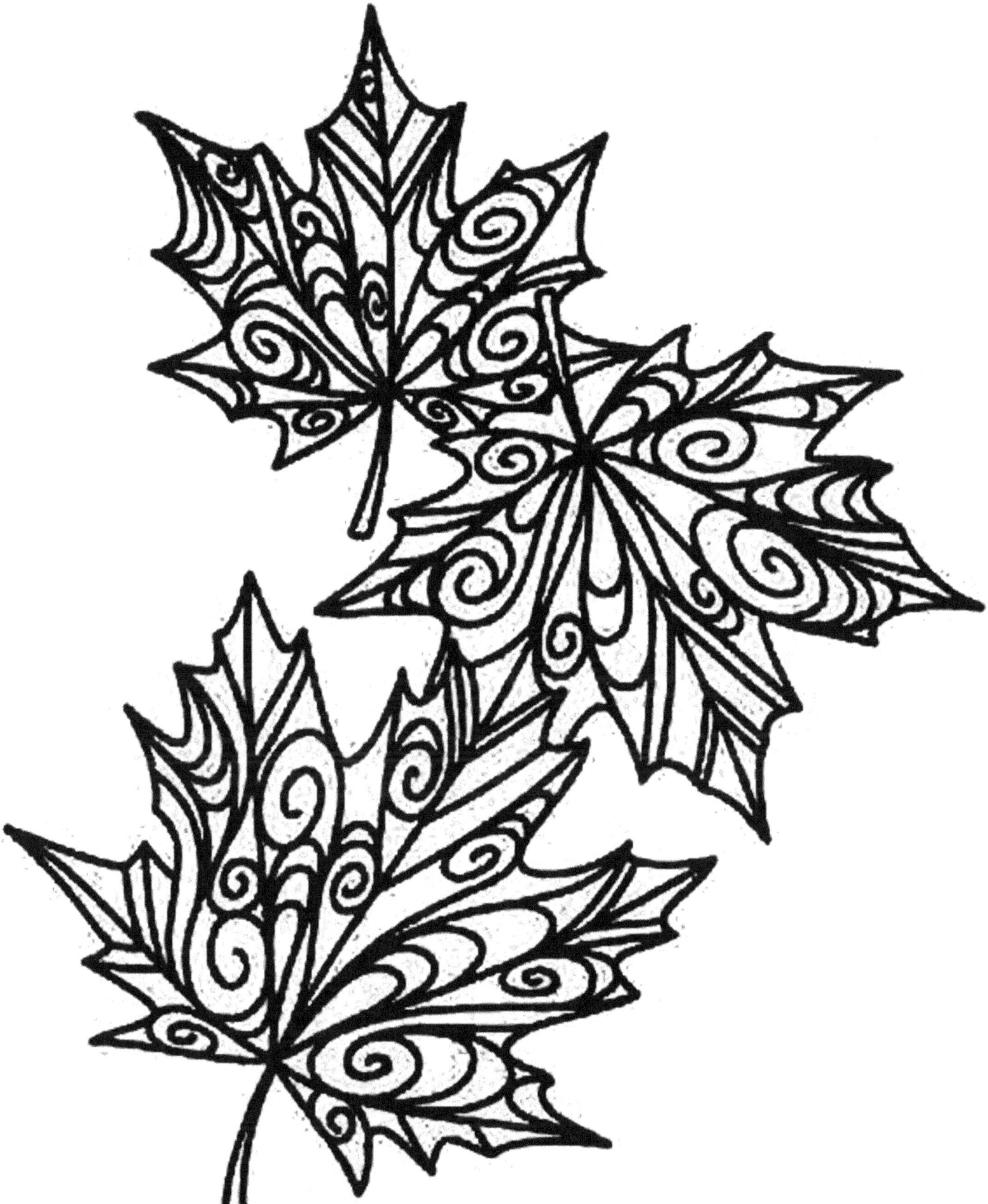

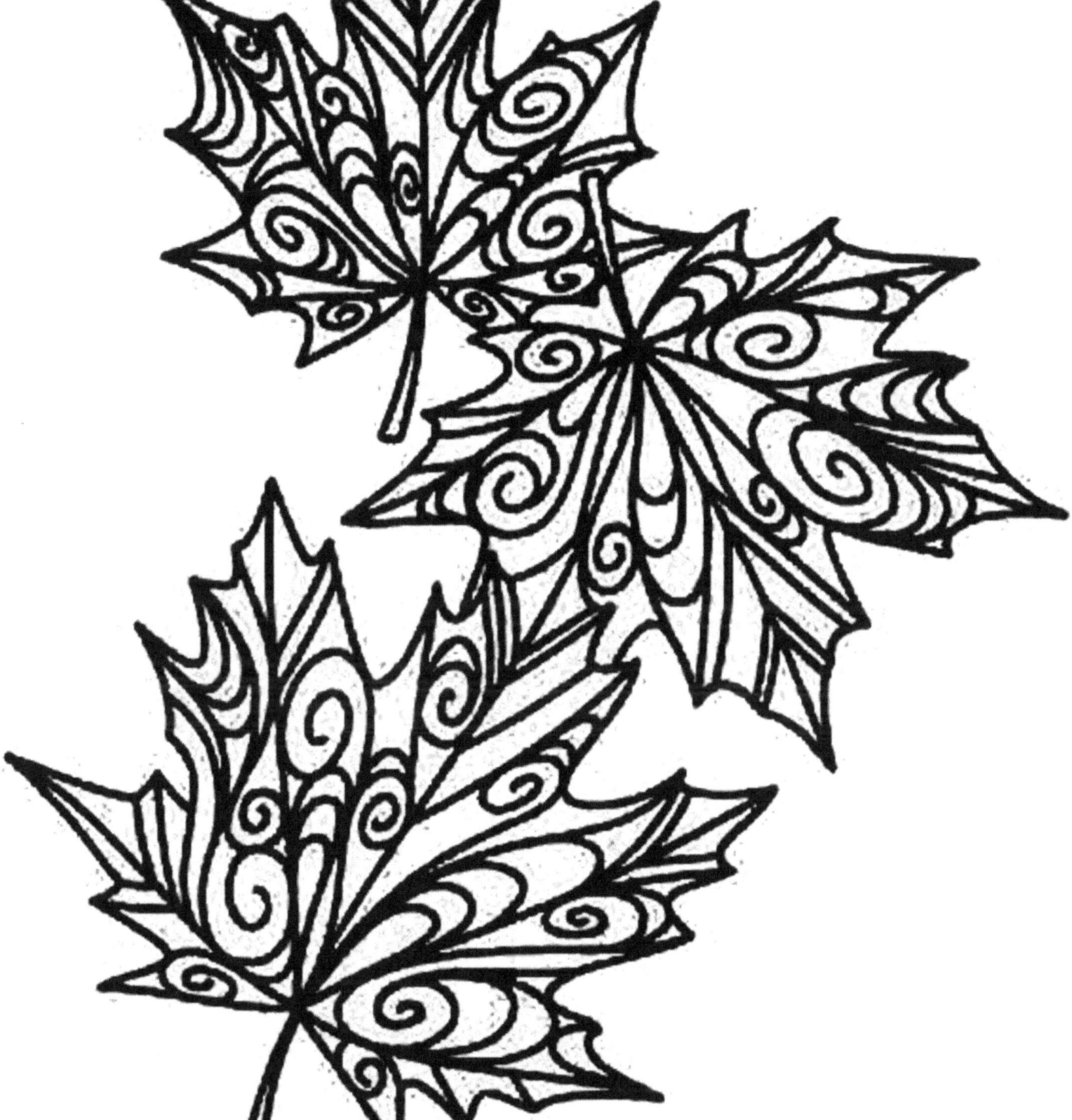

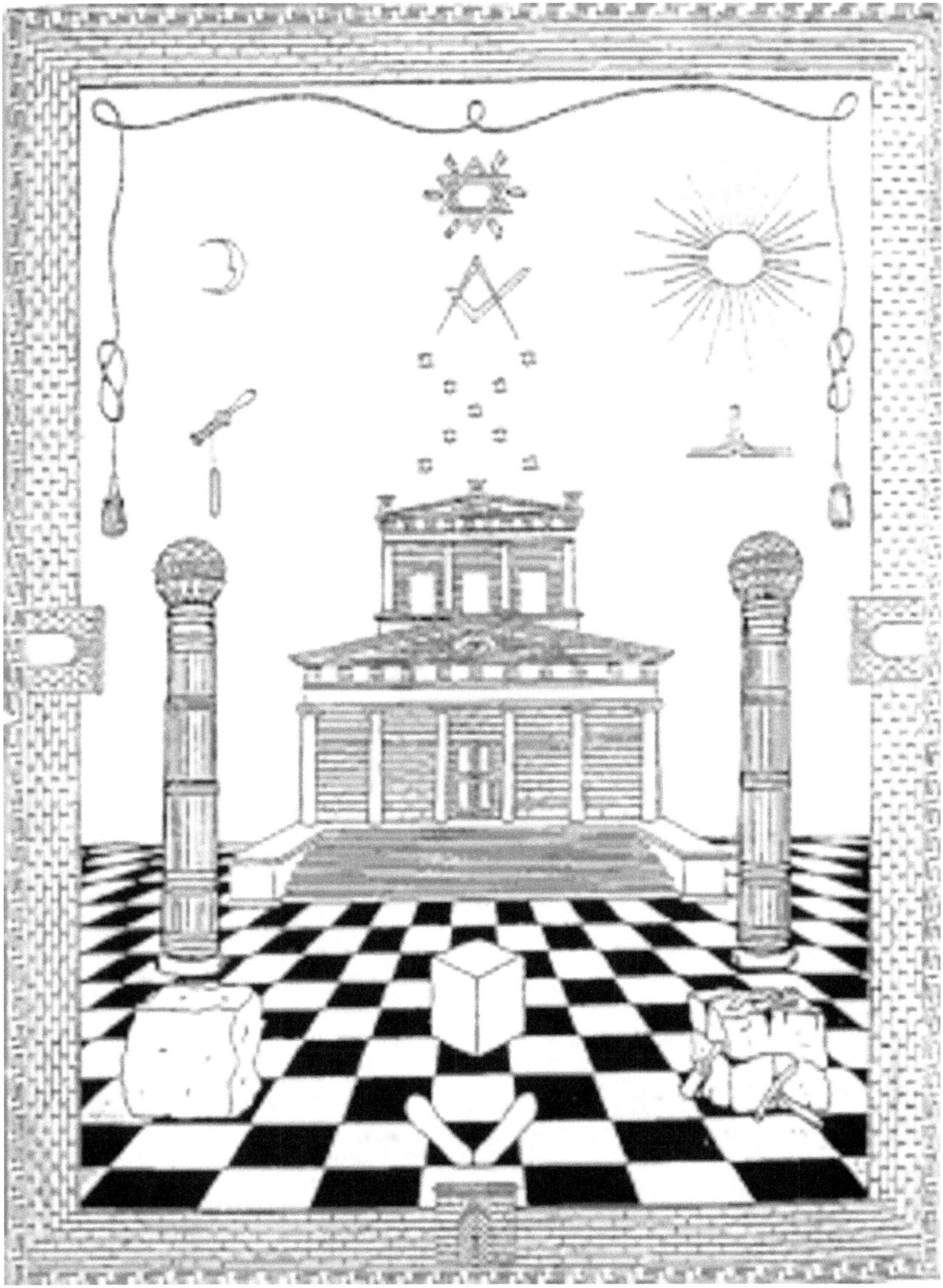

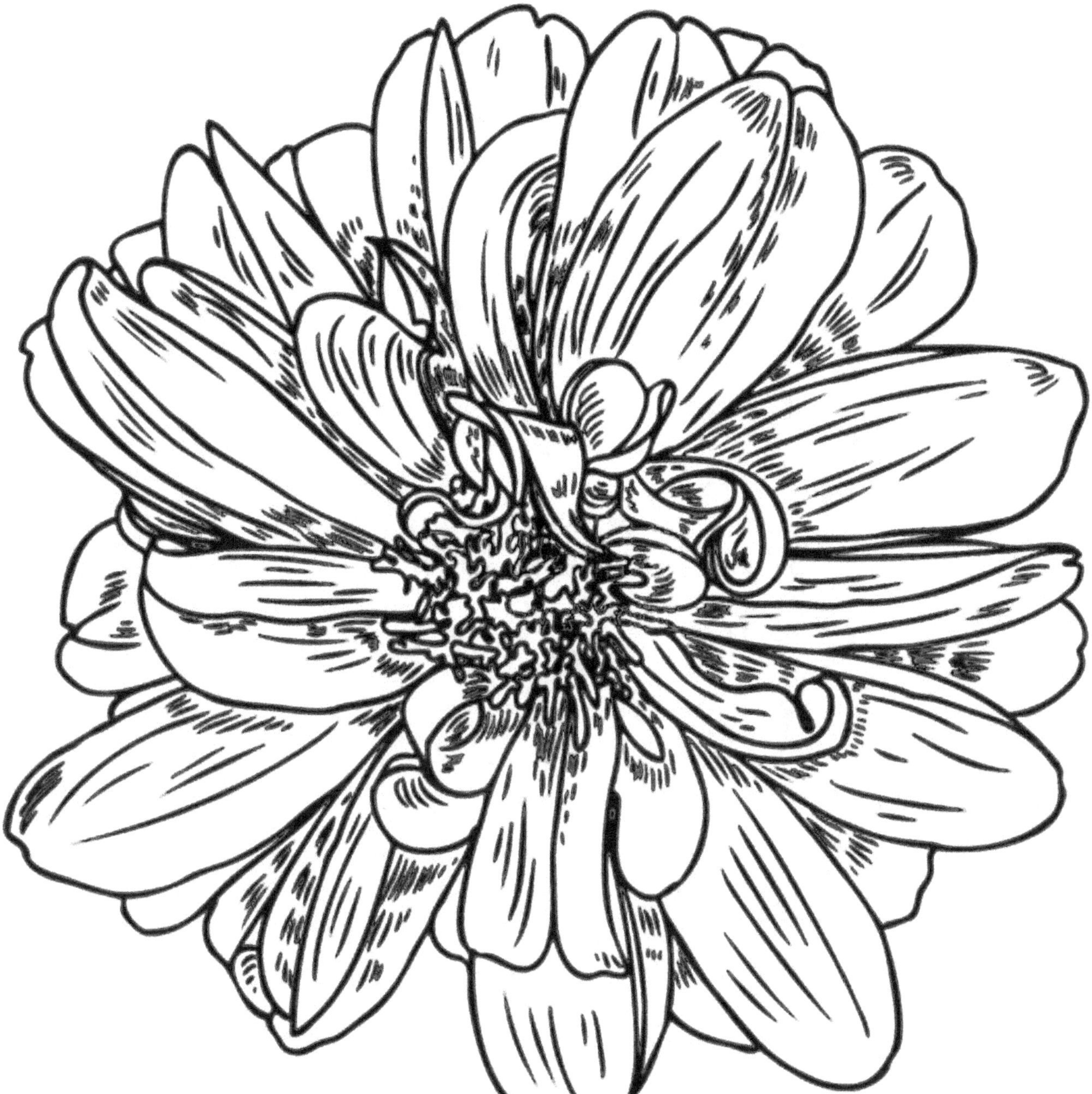

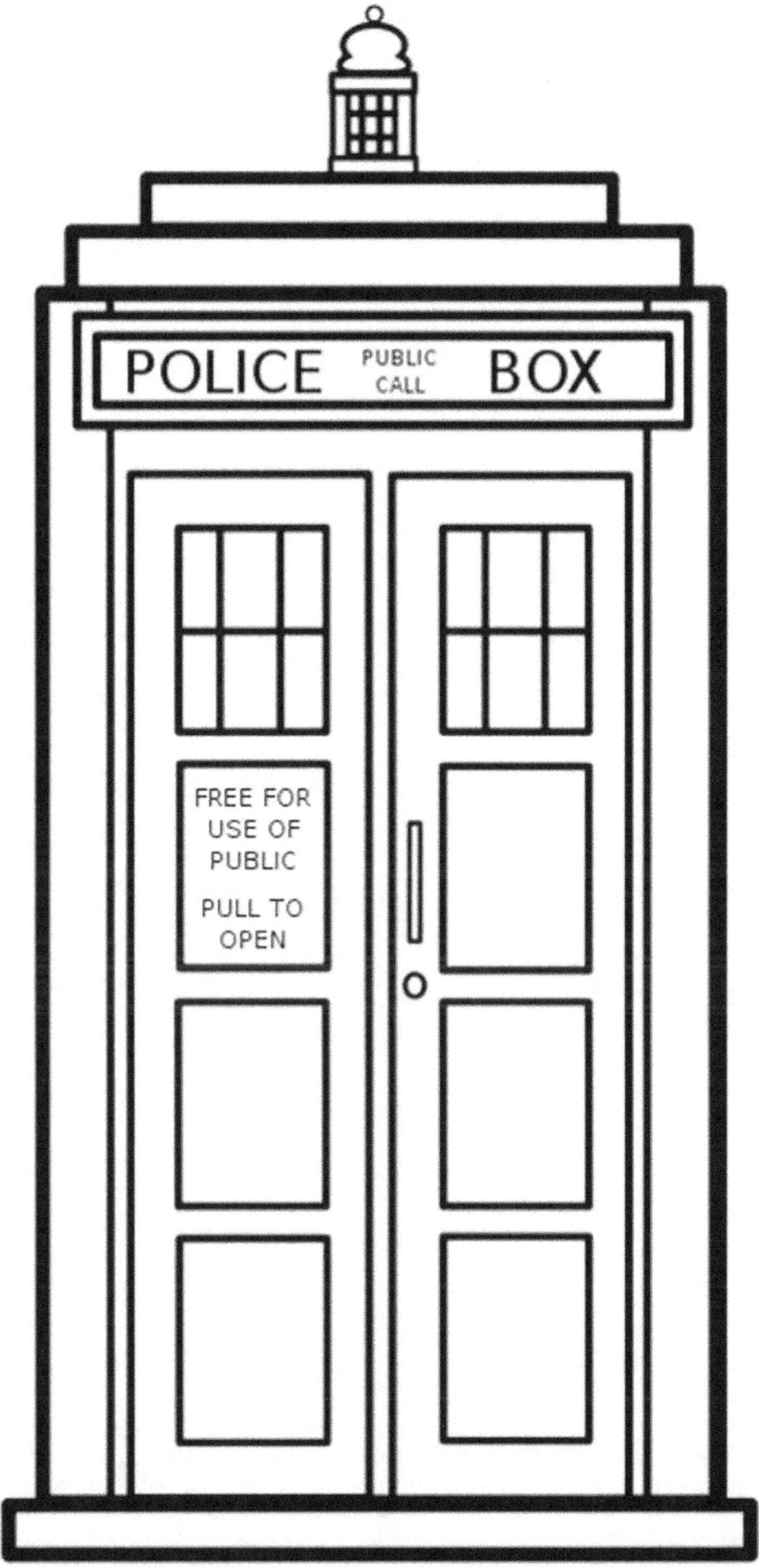
POLICE
PUBLIC CALL
BOX
FREE FOR USE OF PUBLIC
PULL TO OPEN

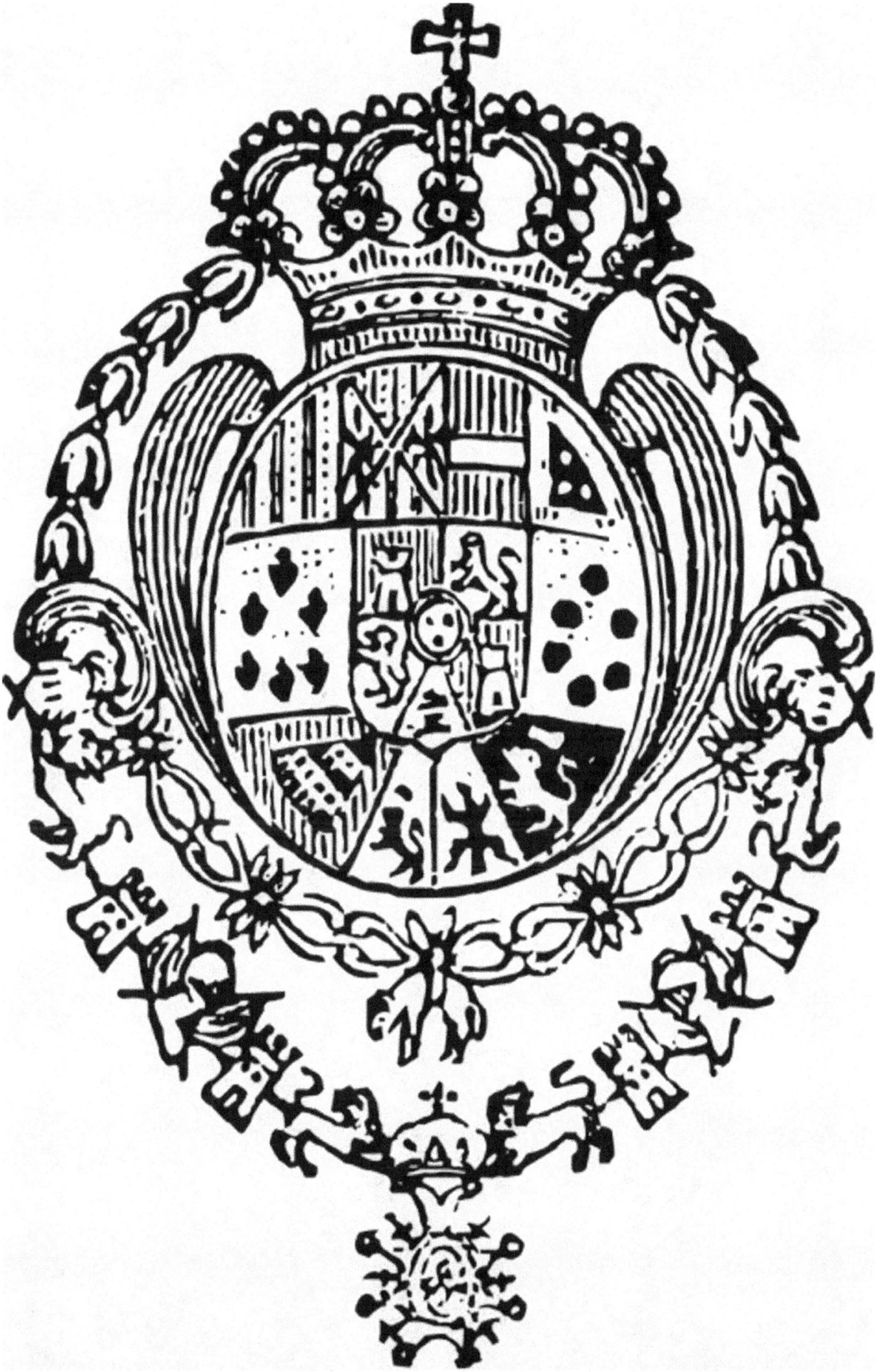

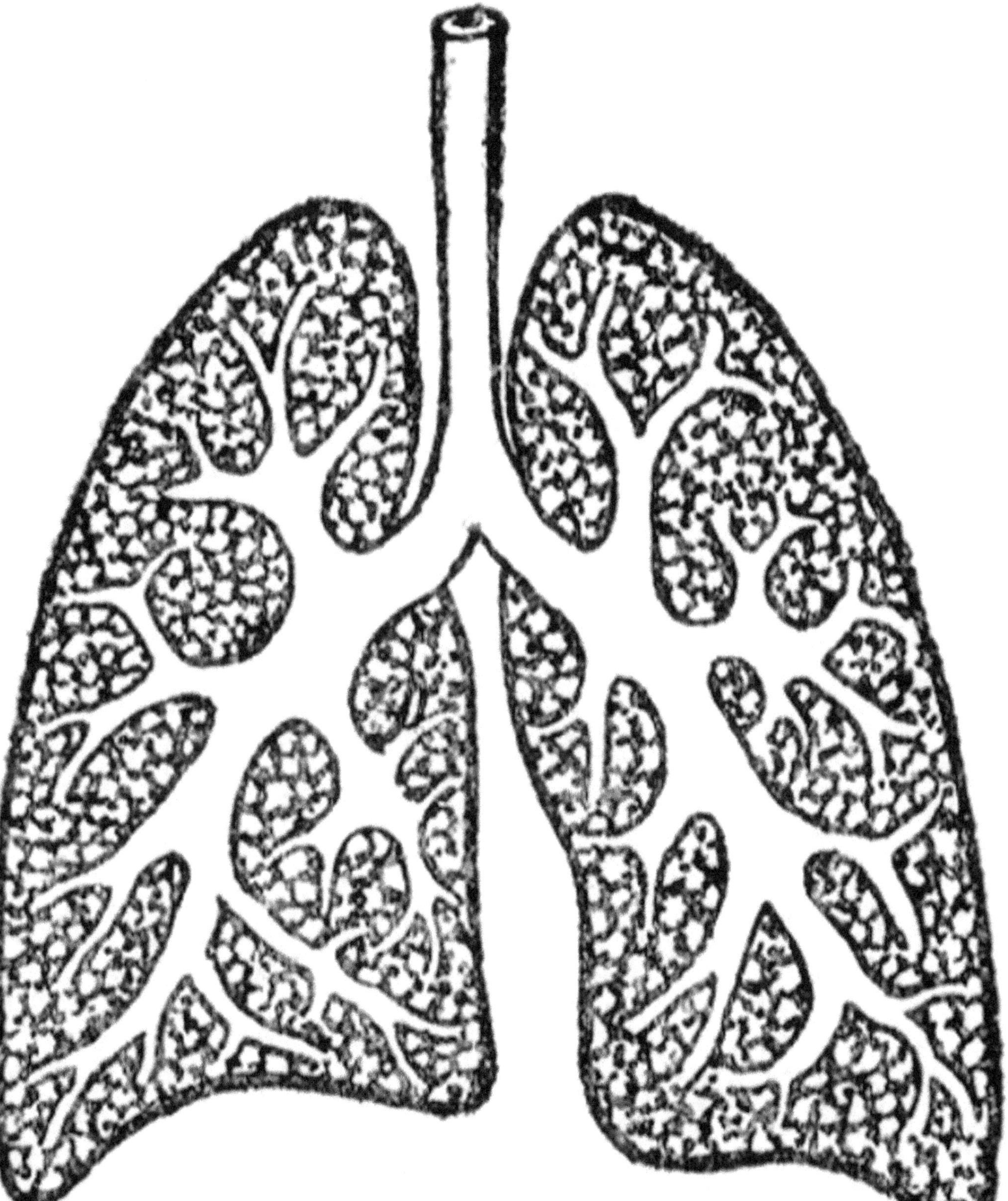

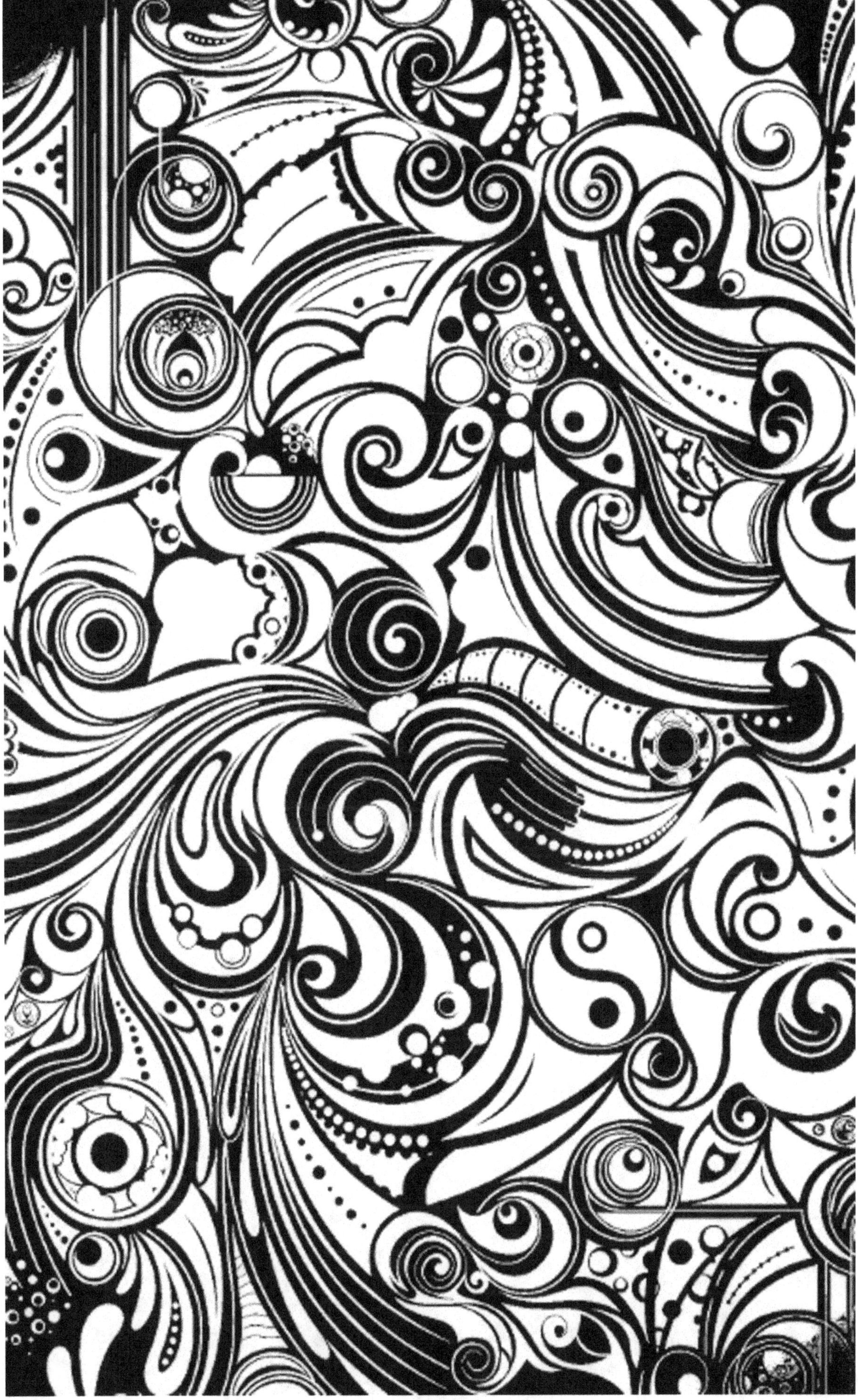

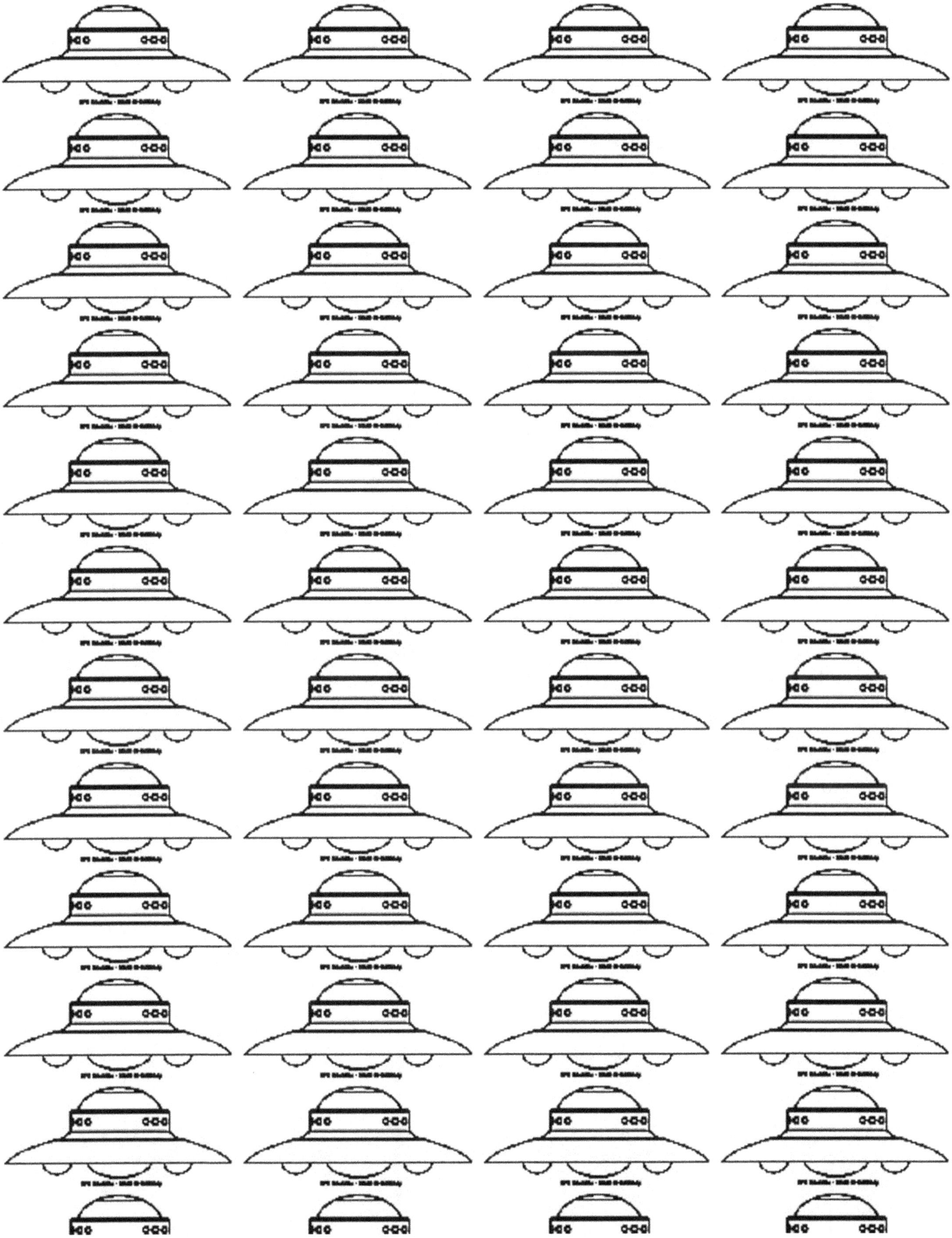

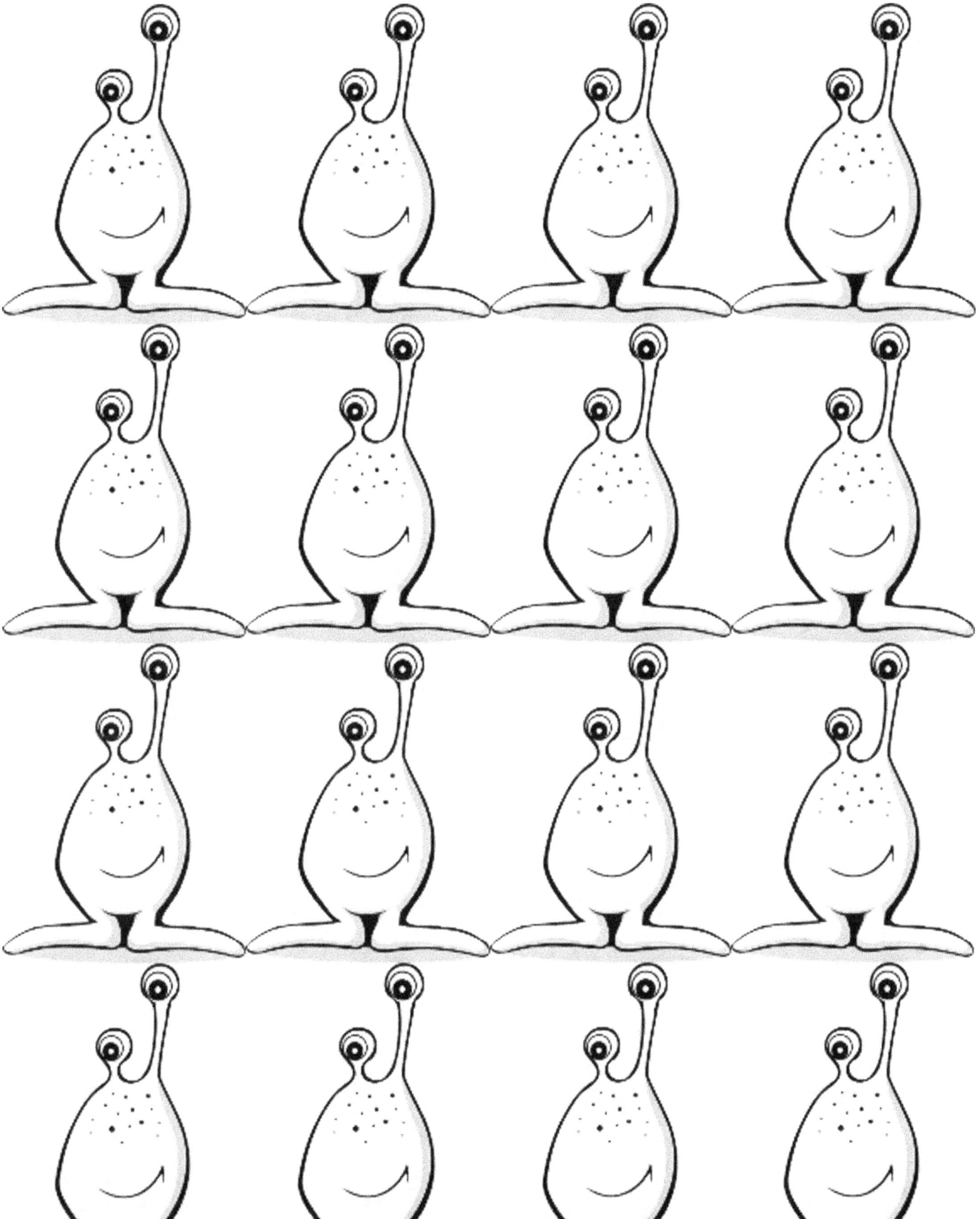

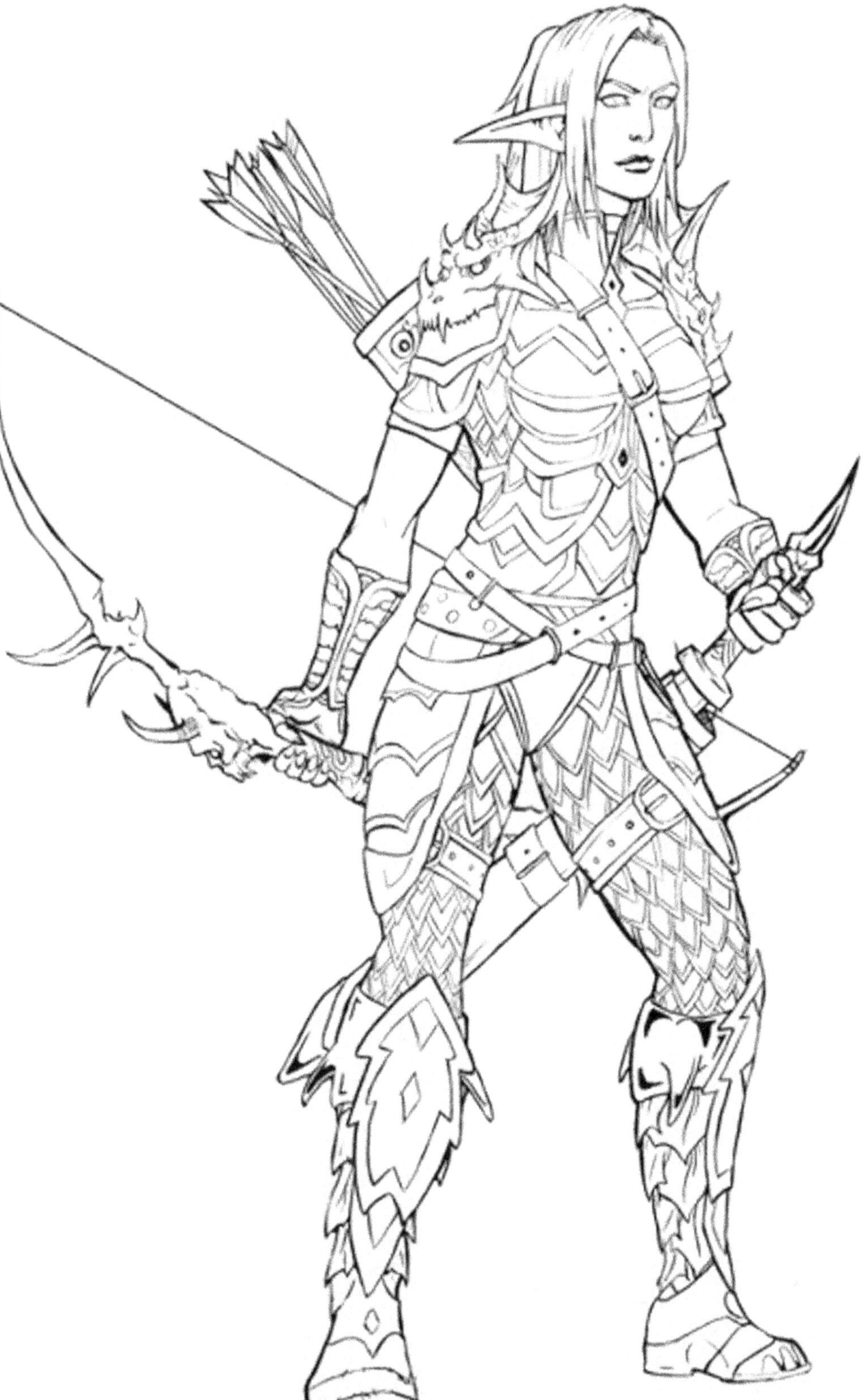

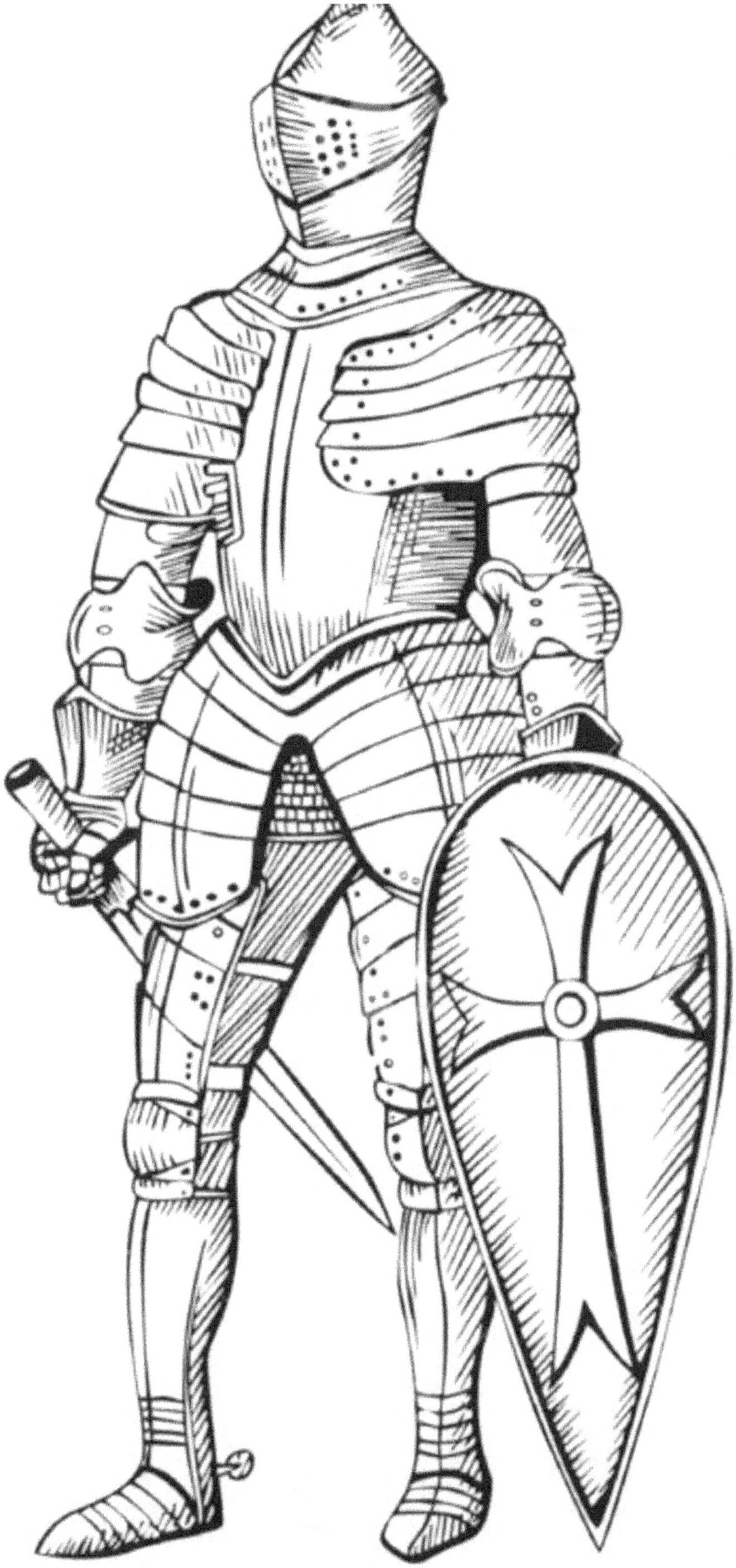

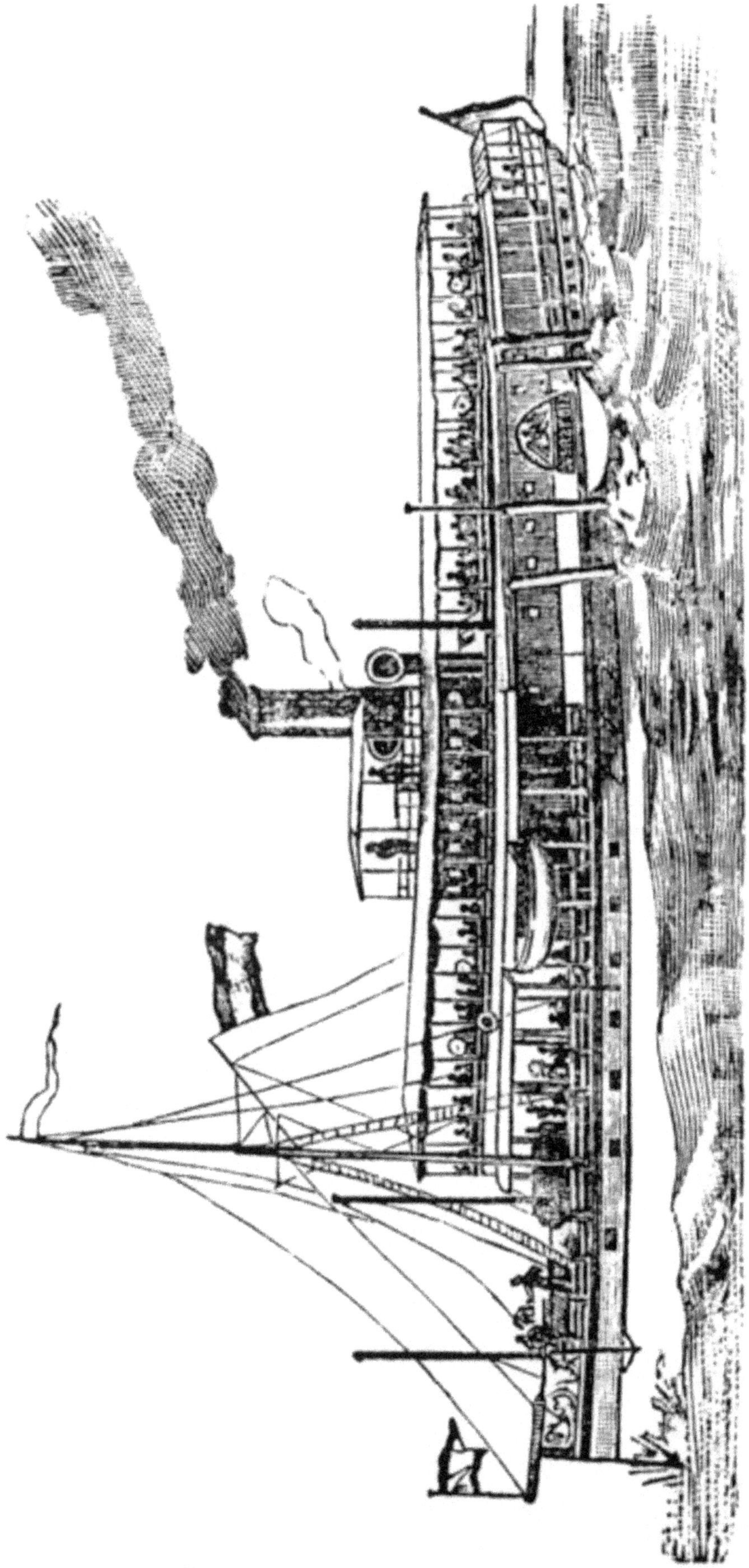

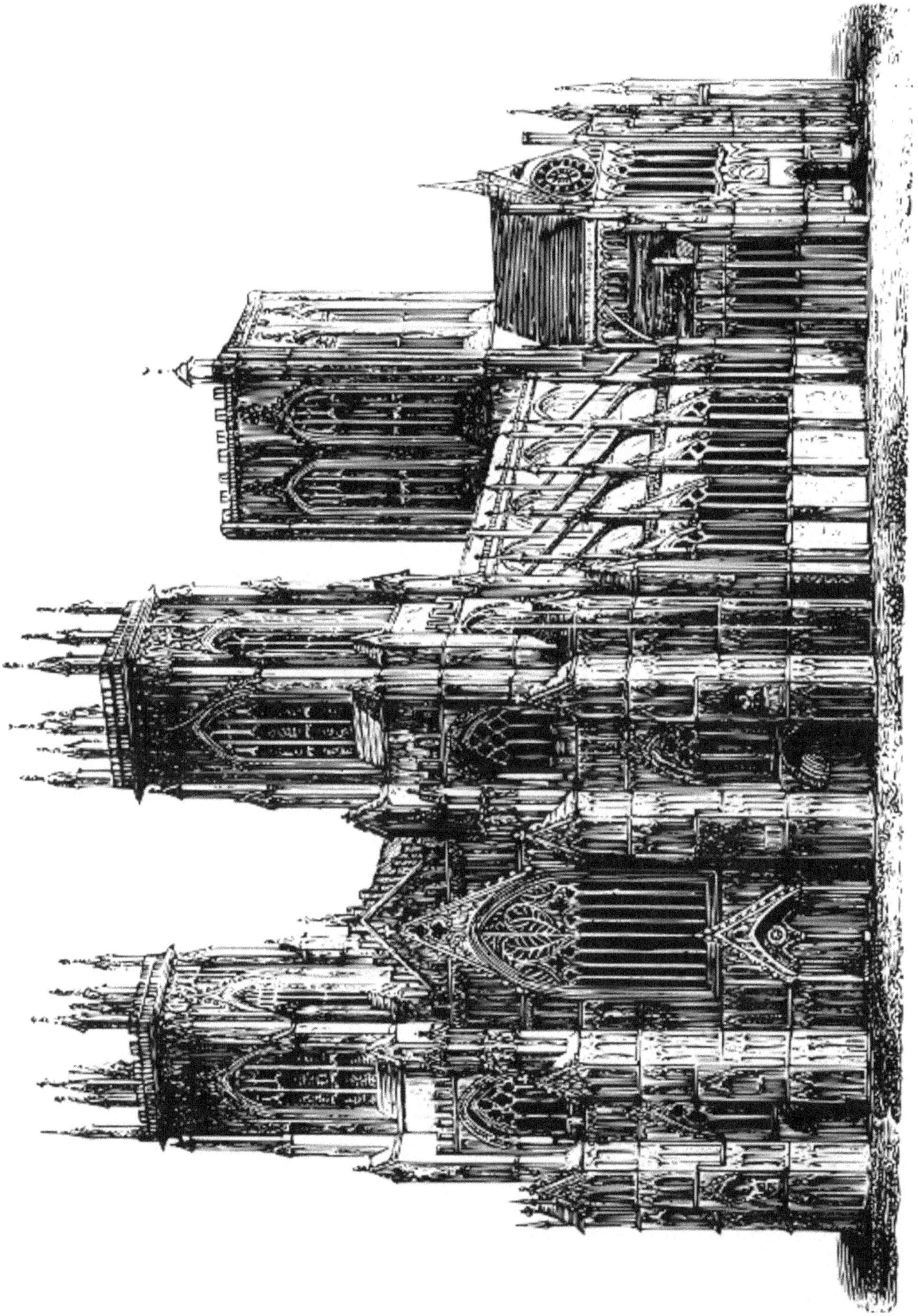

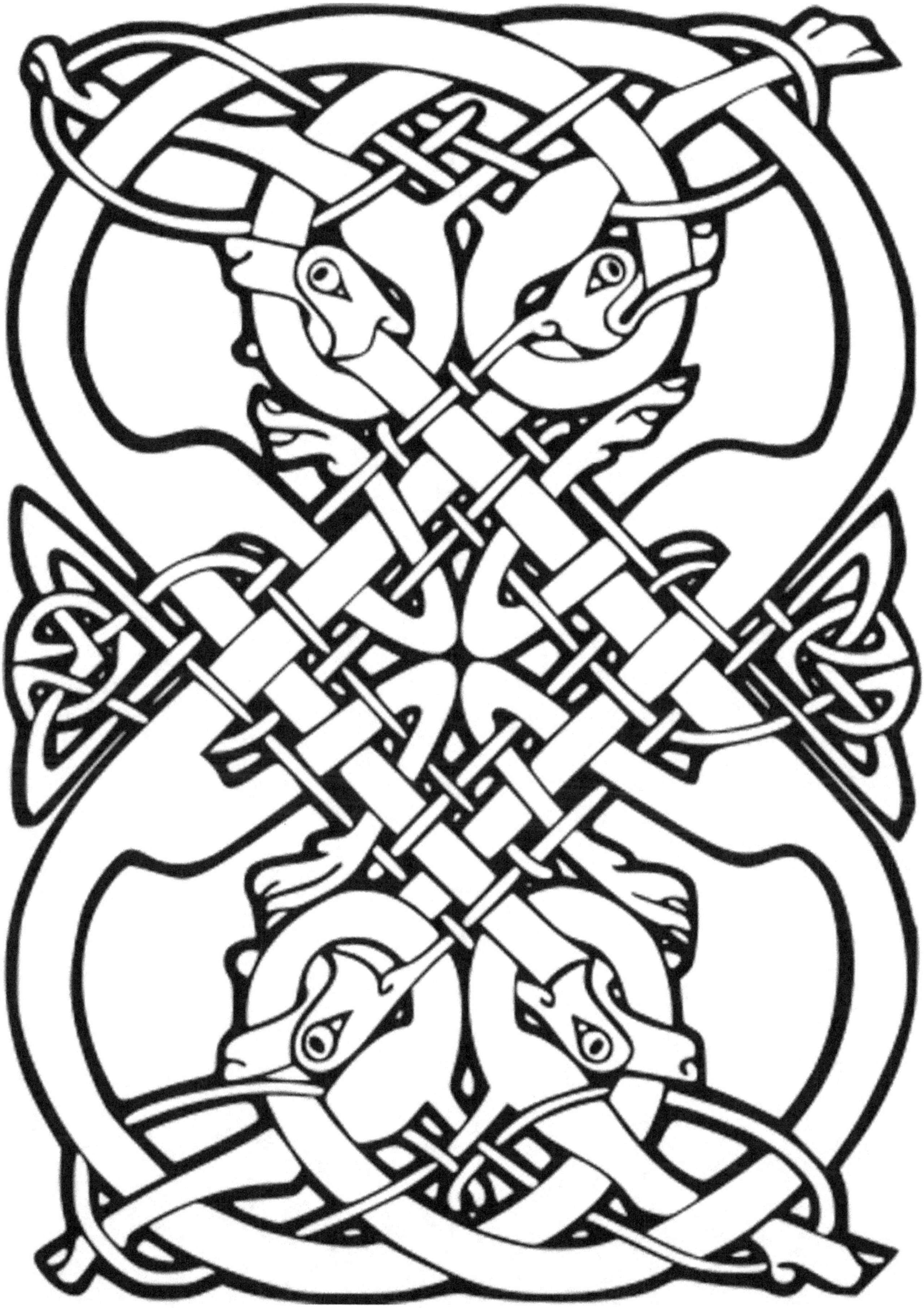

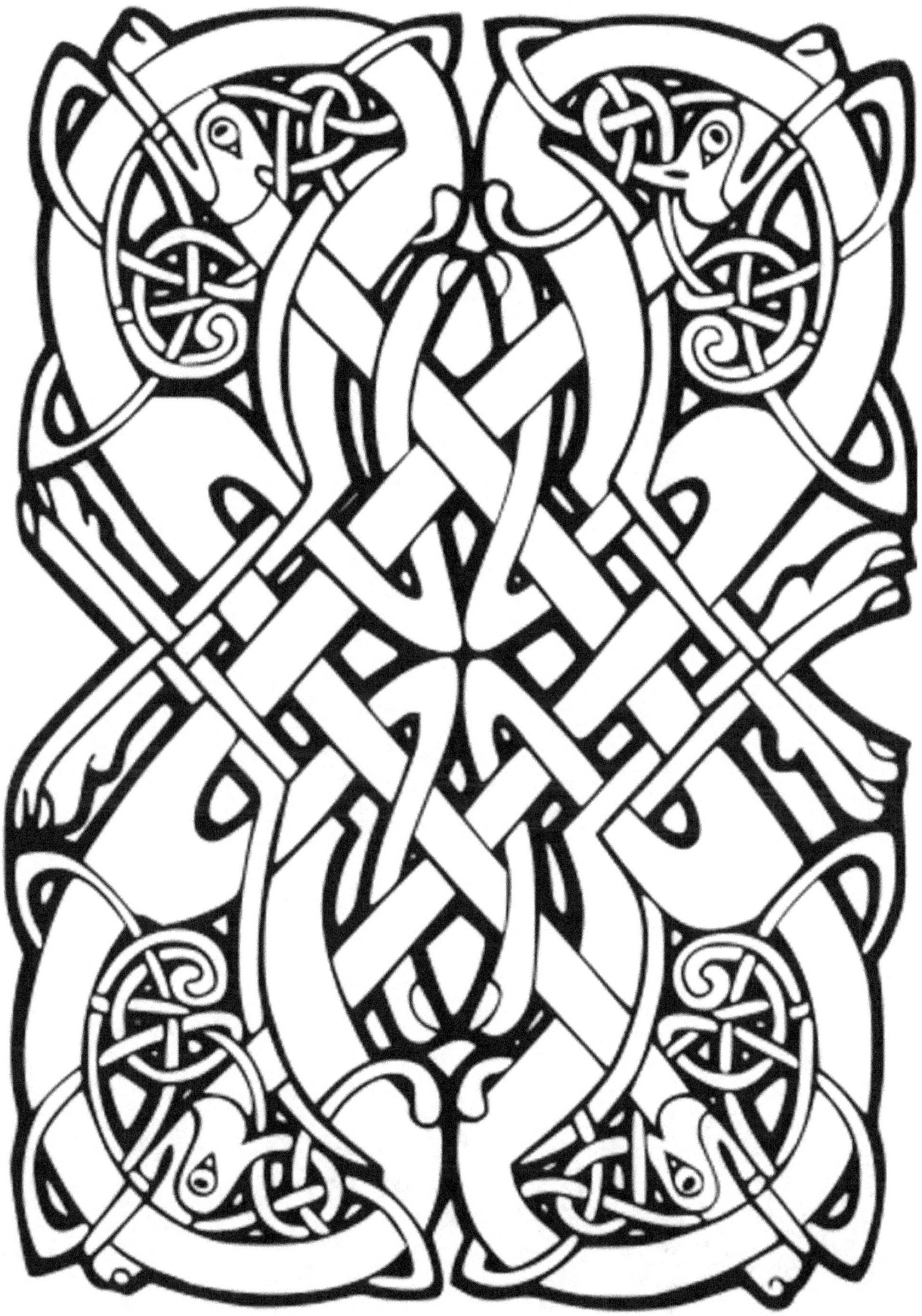

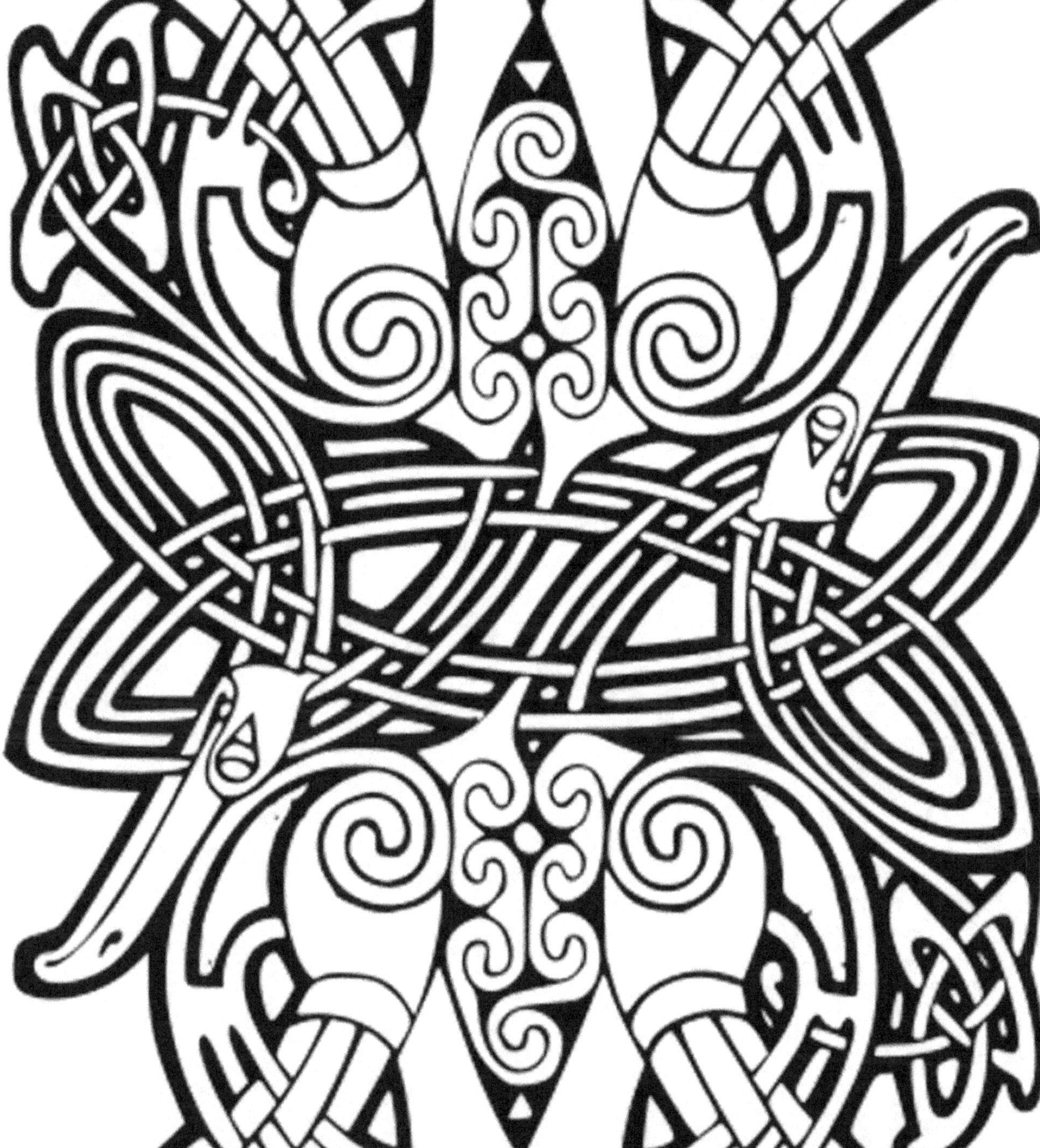

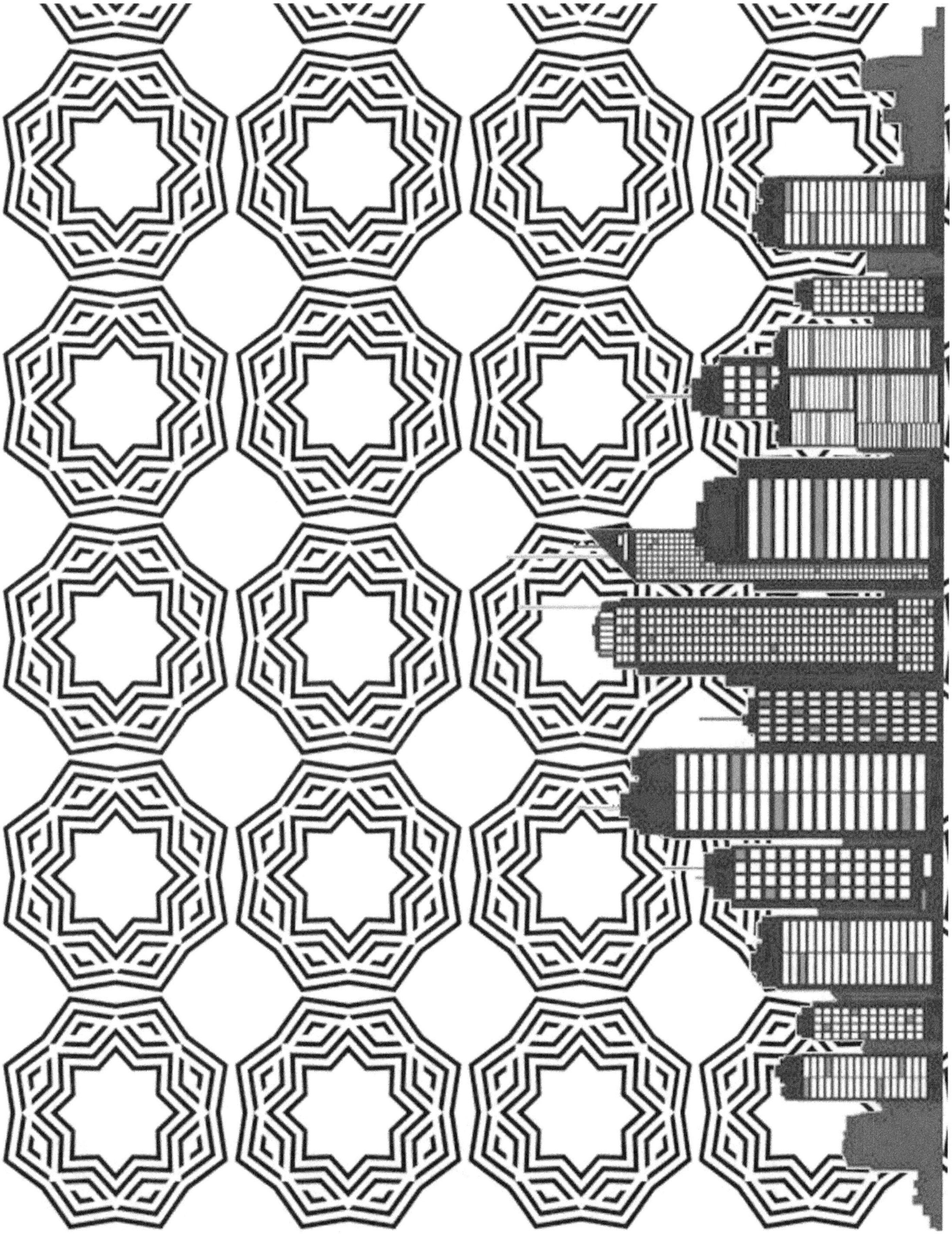

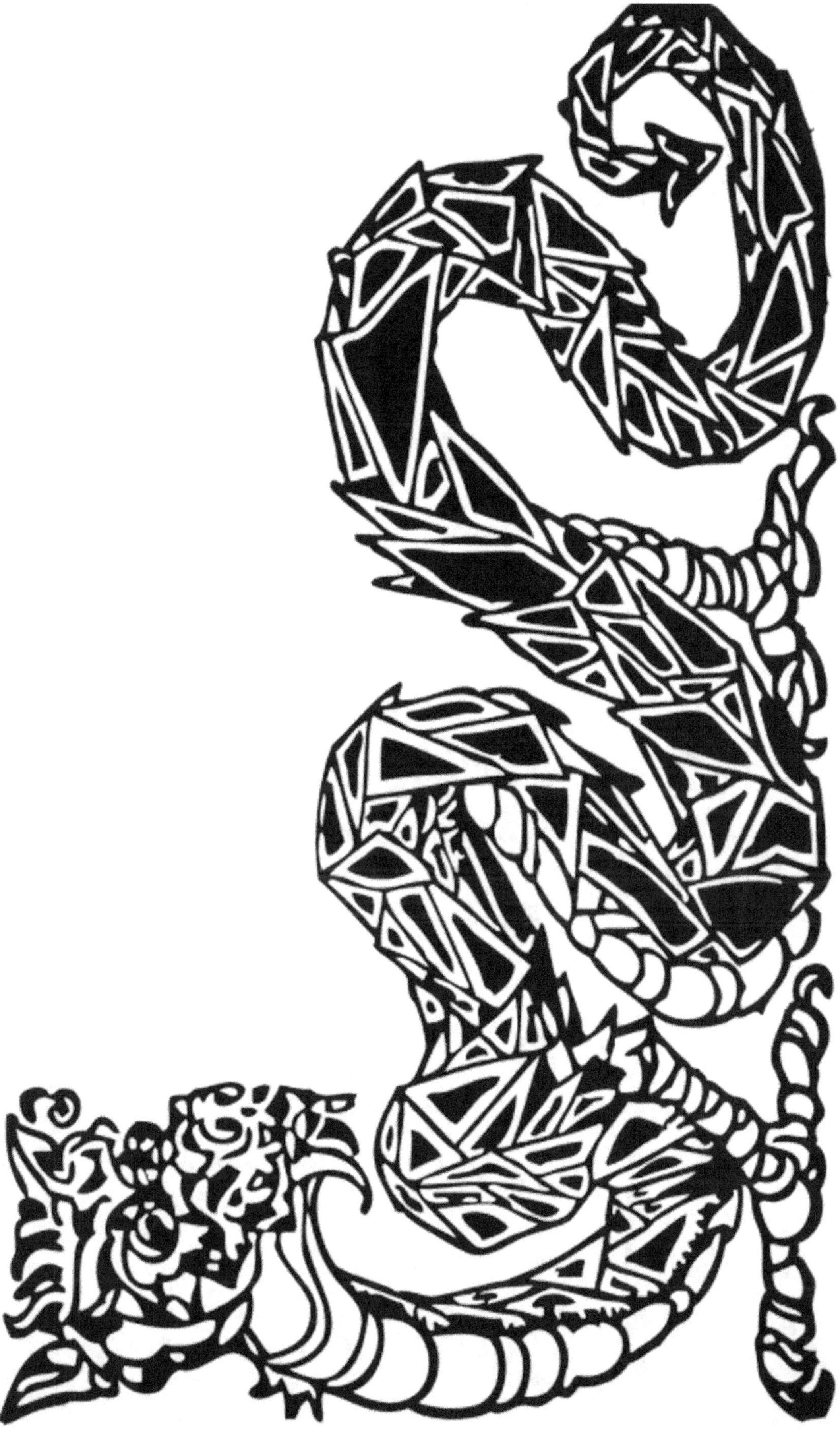

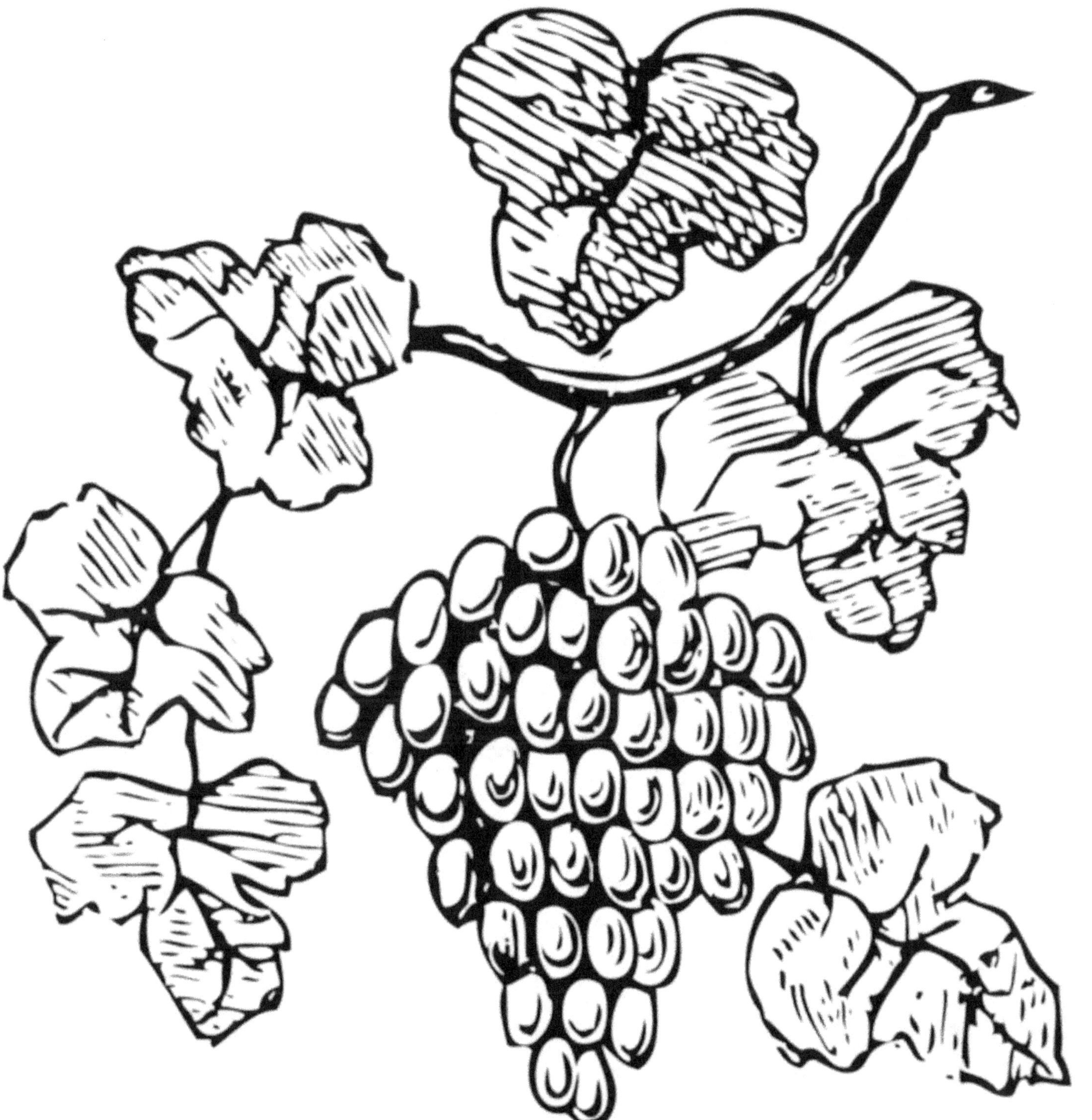

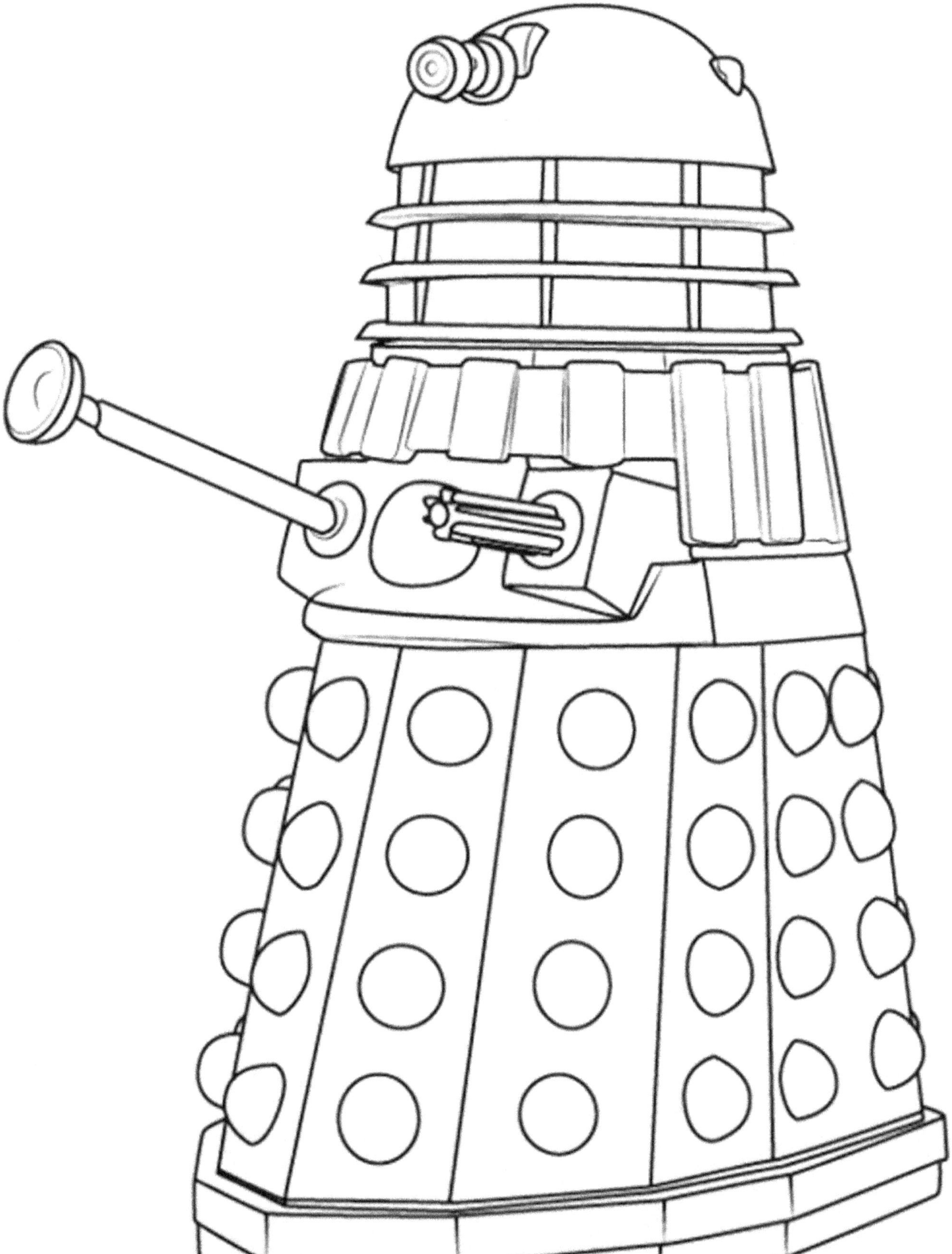

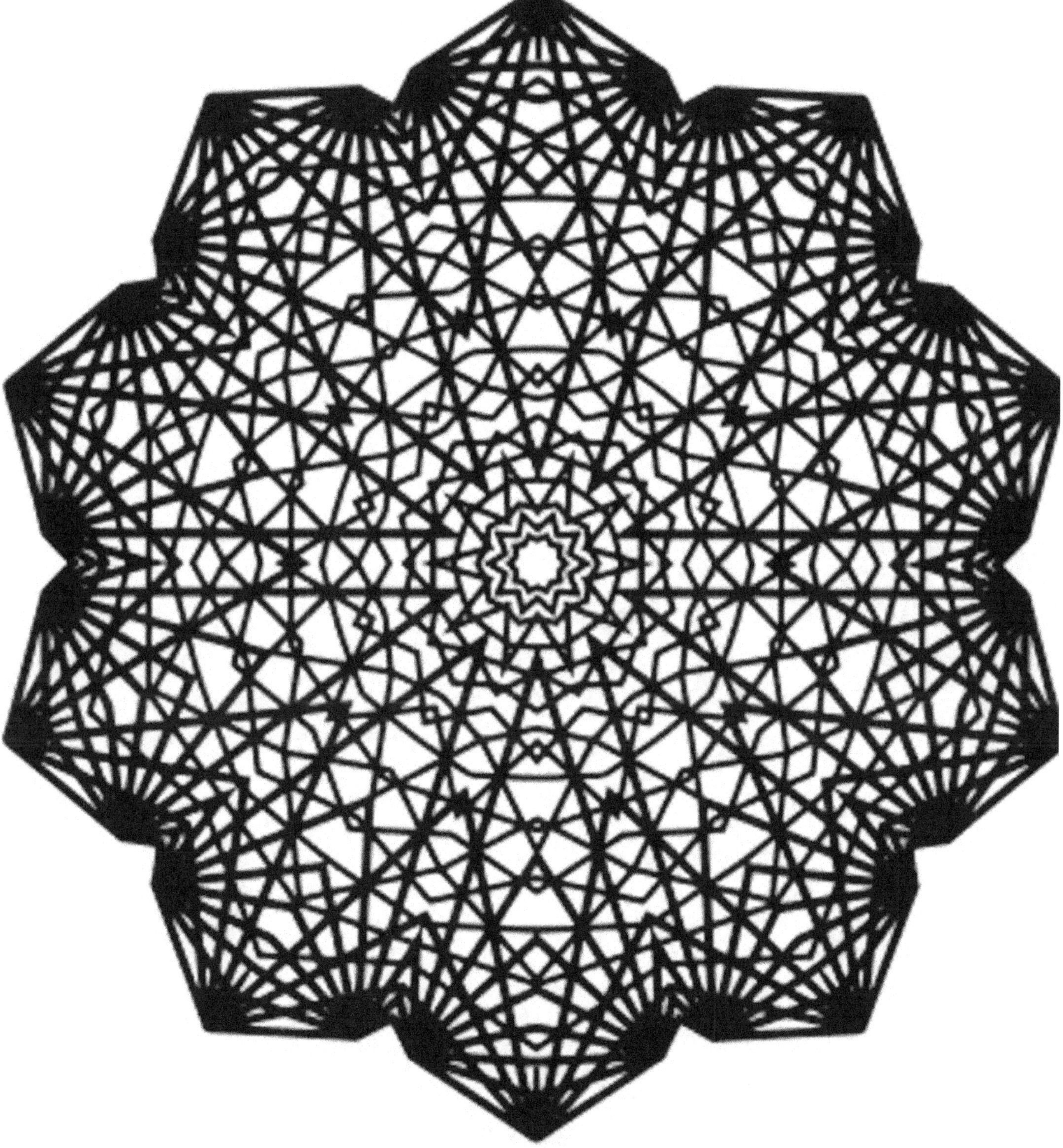

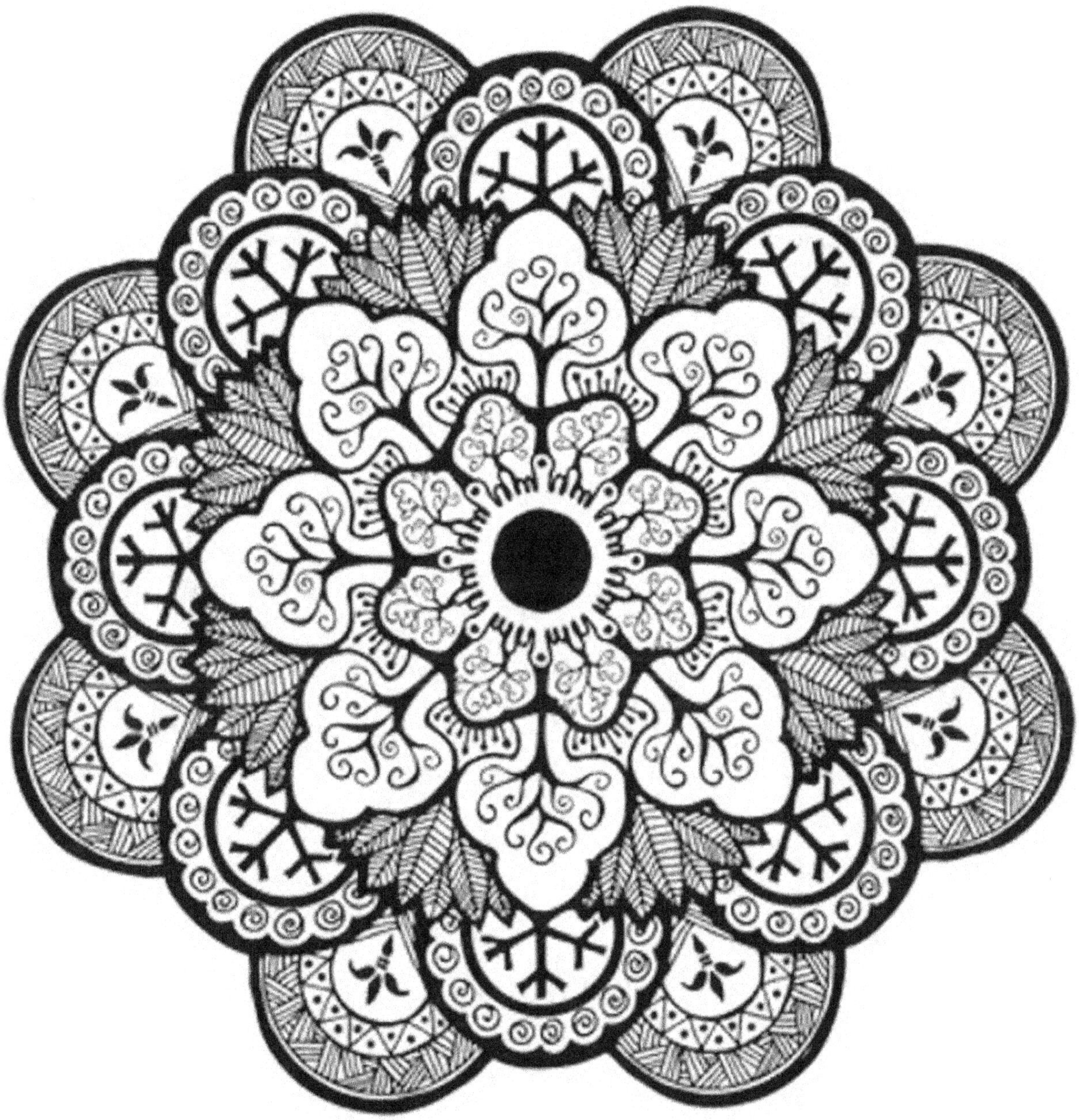

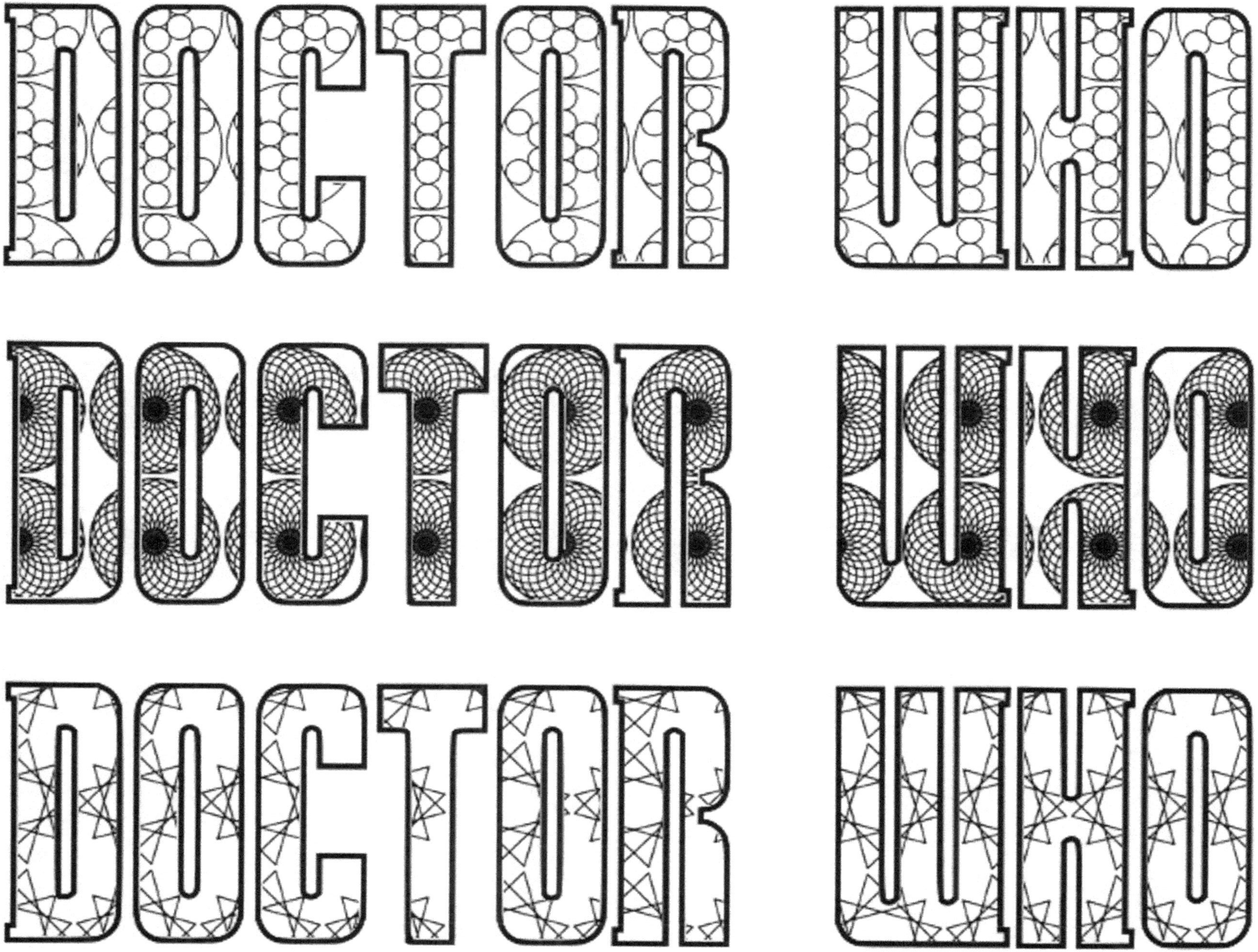
DOCTOR WHO
DOCTOR WHO
DOCTOR WHO

सत्यमेव जयते

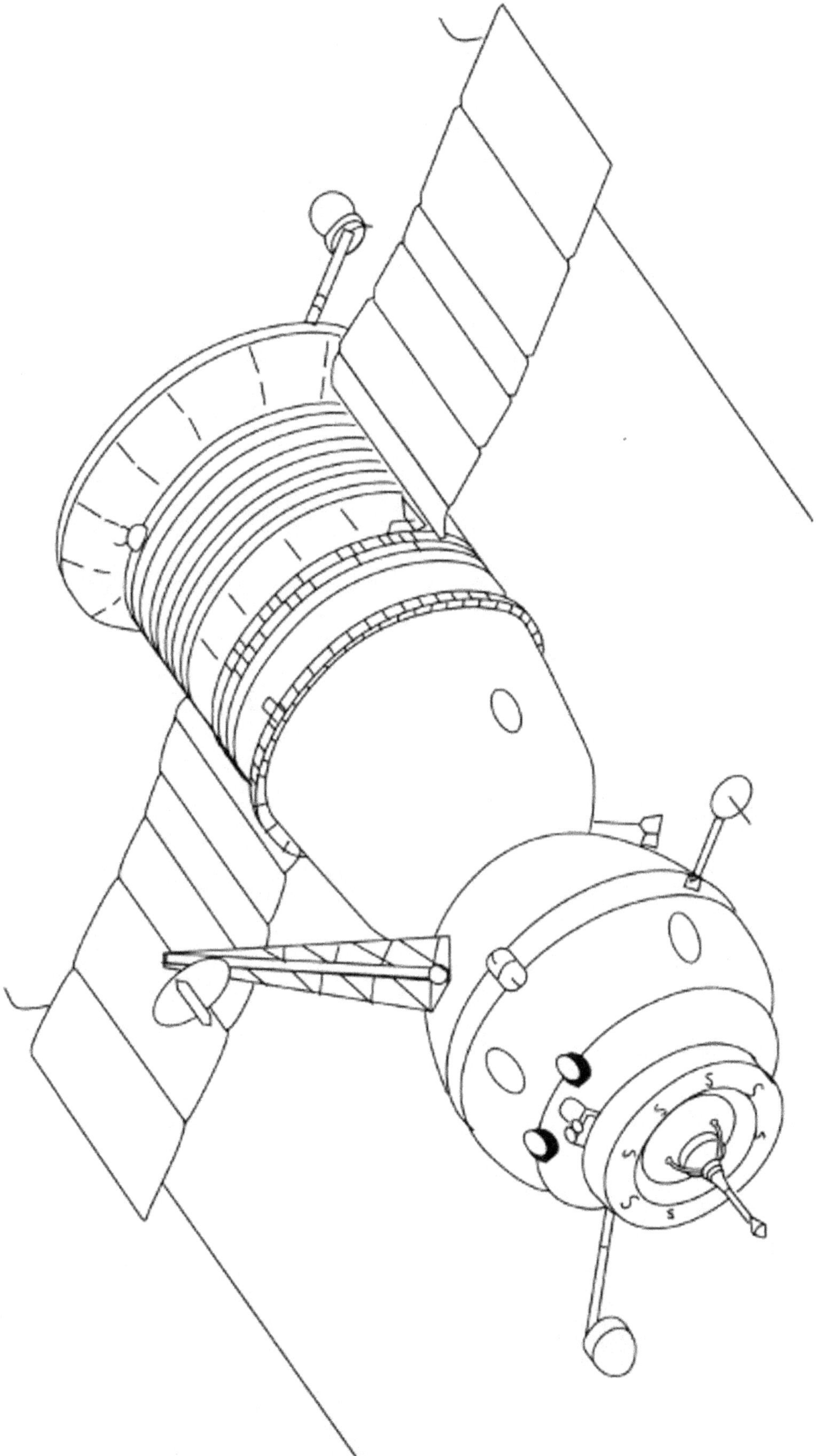

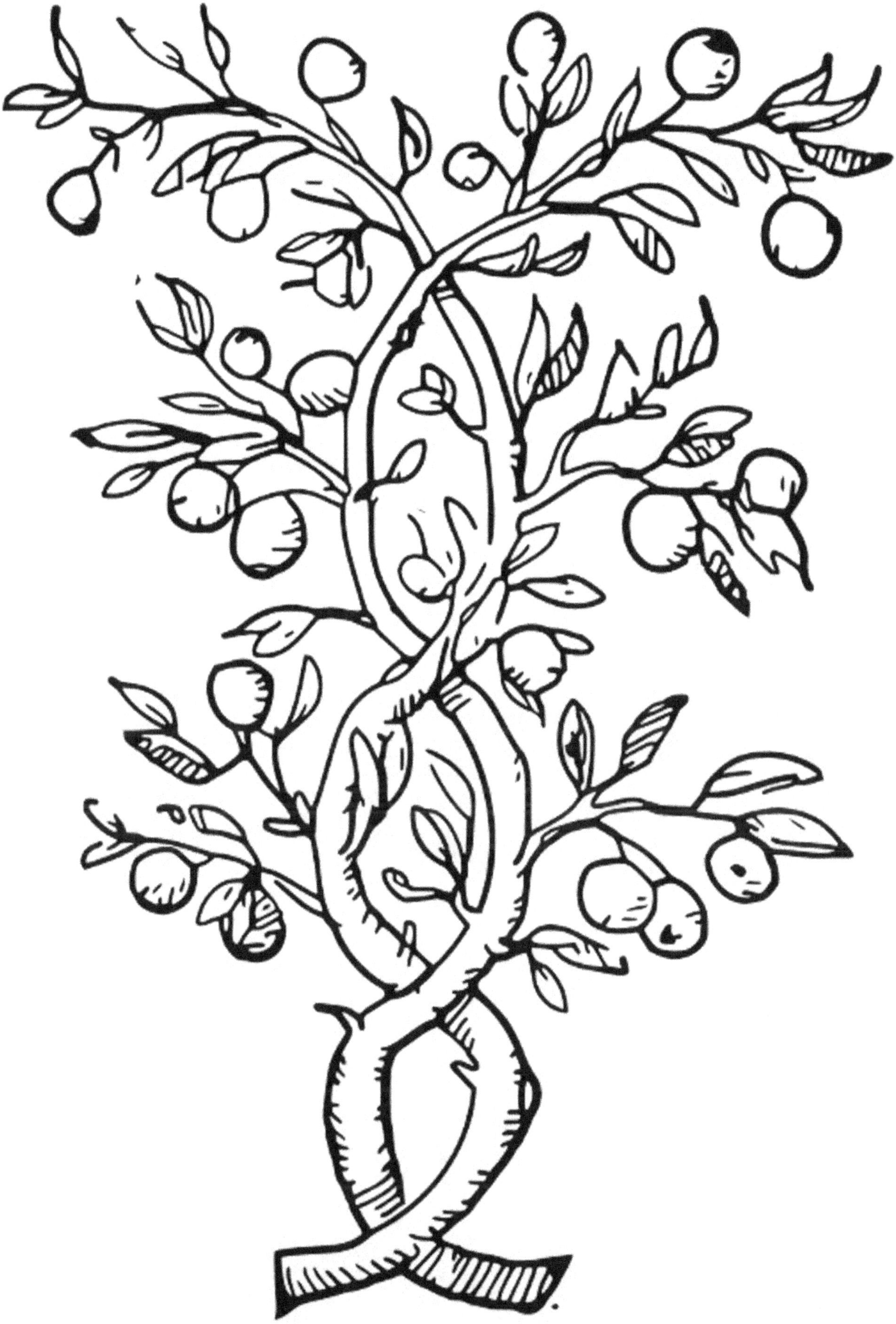

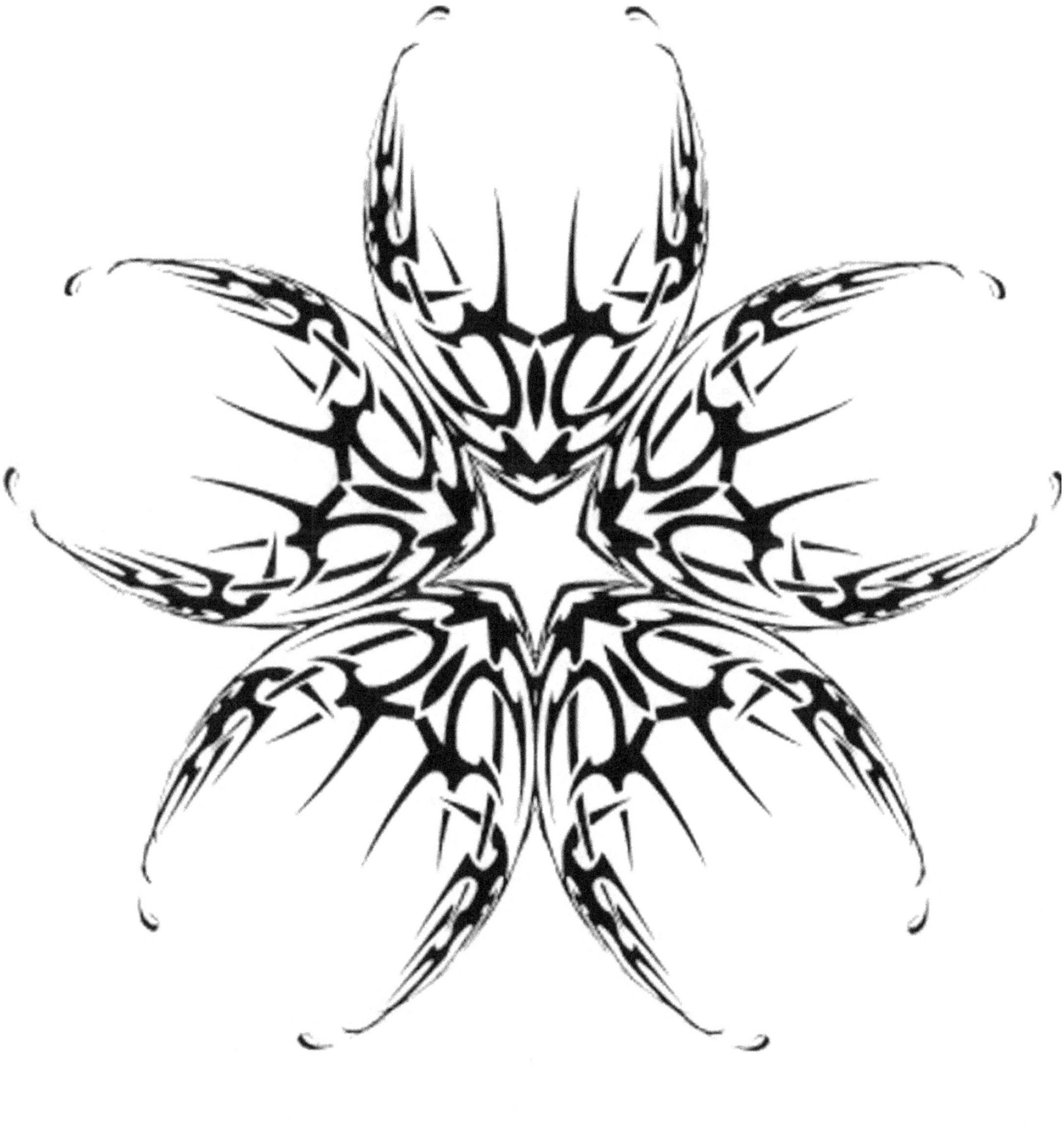

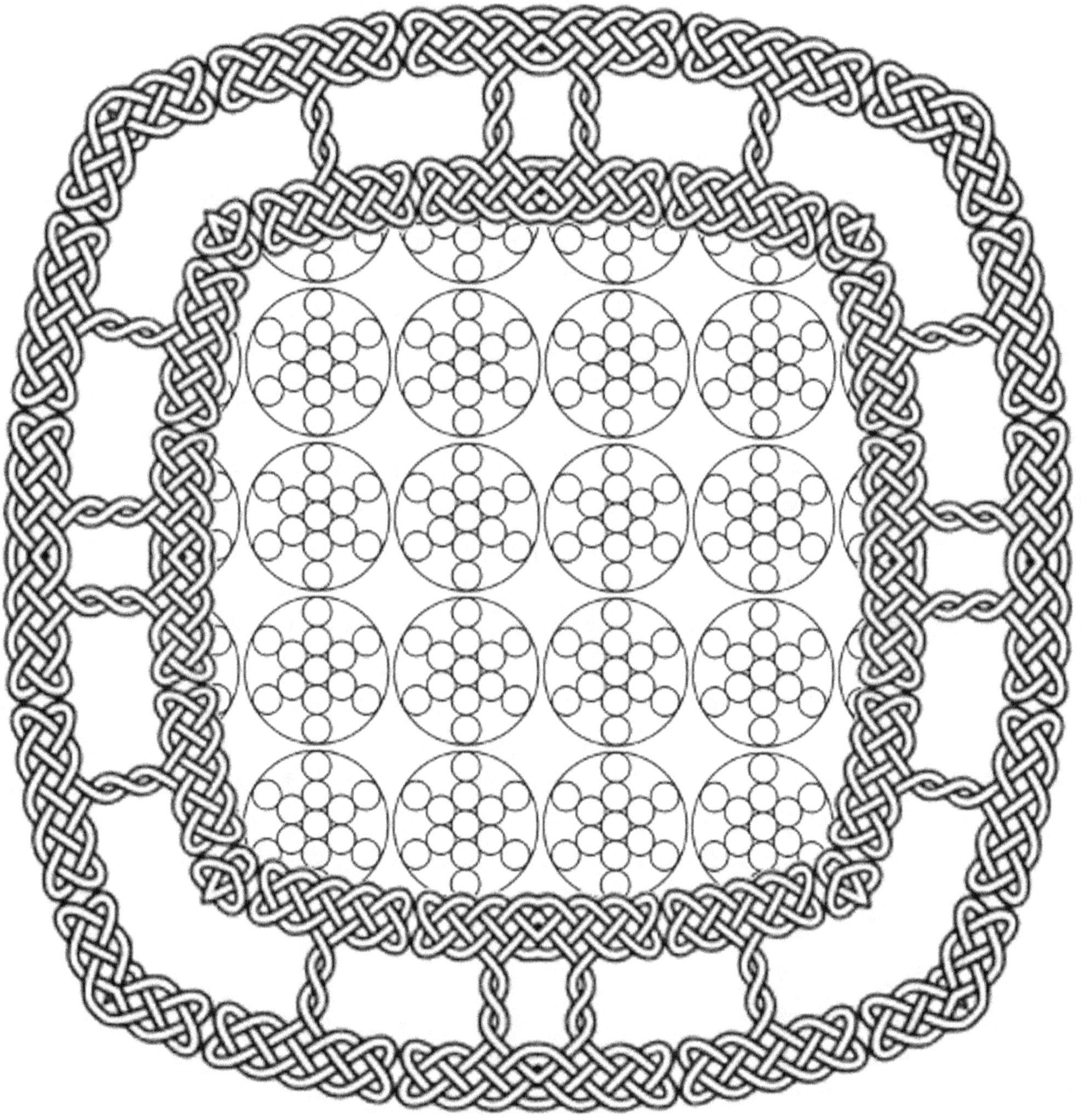

www.ingramcontent.com/pod-product-compliance
Lightning Source LLC
Chambersburg PA
CBHW081747220526
45468CB00008B/2273